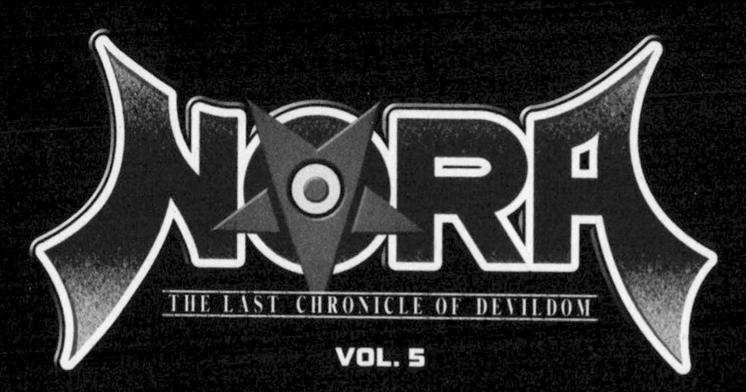

VOL. 5

STORY AND ART BY
KAZUNARI KAKEI

English Adaptation/Park Cooper & Barb Lien-Cooper
Translation/Nori Minami
Touch-up Art & Lettering/Annaliese Christman
Design/Sam Elzway
Editor/Shaenon K. Garrity

Editor in Chief, Books/Alvin Lu
Editor in Chief, Magazines/Marc Weidenbaum
VP, Publishing Licensing/Rika Inouye
VP, Sales & Product Marketing/Gonzalo Ferreyra
VP, Creative/Linda Espinosa
Publisher/Hyoe Narita

Printed in the U.S.A.

Published by VIZ Media, LLC
P.O. Box 77010
San Francisco, CA 94107

10 9 8 7 6 5 4 3 2 1
First printing, June 2009

www.viz.com

www.shonenjump.com

Made by Shibayan (from paper clay)

Kazunari Kakei

Lately it takes about half a month to do the artwork in *Nora*. I spend the other half of the month on rough drafts, but it doesn't always go smoothly. I battle against paper and pen every day. In the end, not only do I lose sleep from stress, I have to pull consecutive all-nighters. Hmmm...making manga is hard.

NORA: The Last Chronicle of Devildom is Kazunari Kakei's first manga series. It debuted in the April 2004 issue of *Monthly Shonen Jump* and eventually spawned a second series, *SUREBREC: NORA the 2nd*, which premiered in *Monthly Shonen Jump*'s March 2007 issue.

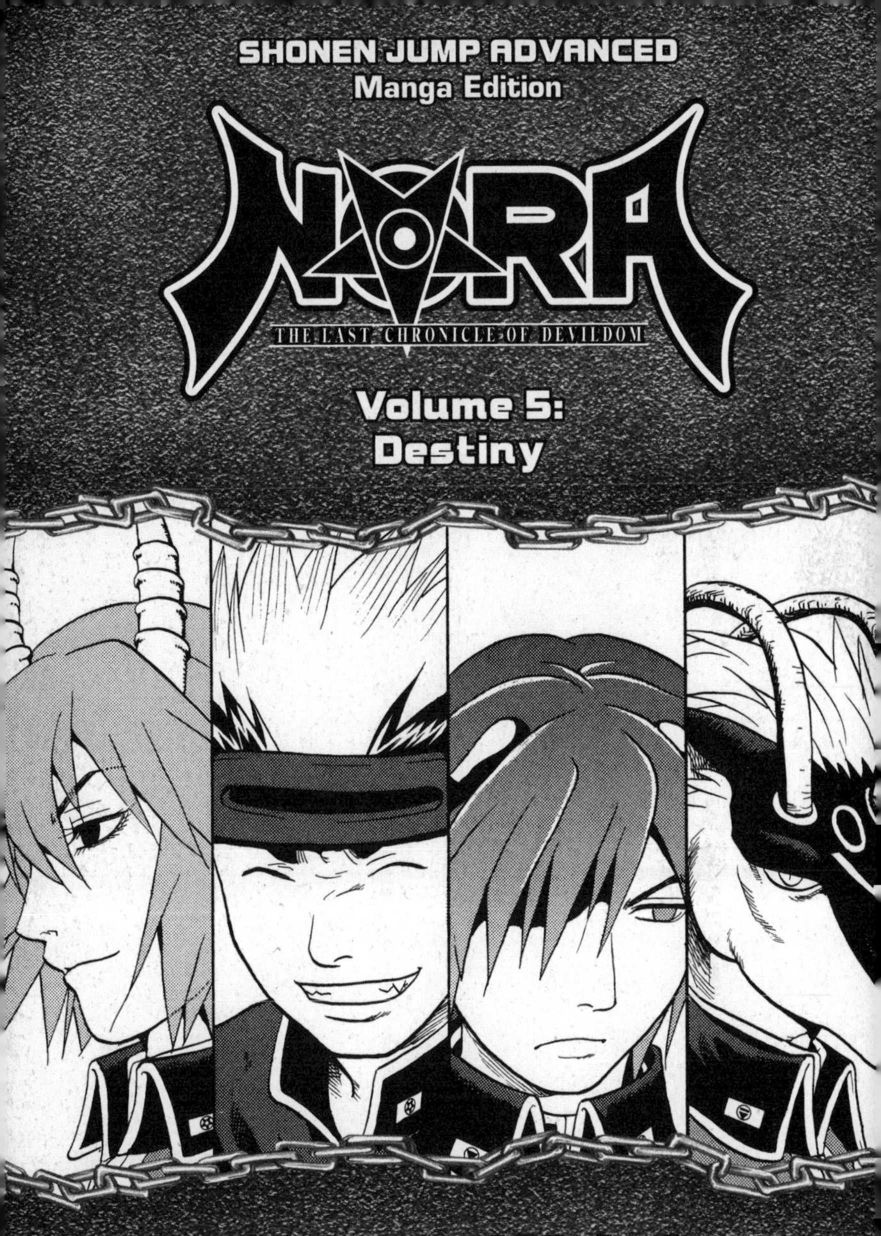

Kazunari Kakei

OUR DEVILISH CAST

KAZUMA (KAZUMA MAGARI)

KAZUMA SEEMS TO HAVE IT ALL. HE'S THE PRESIDENT OF THE STUDENT COUNCIL AS WELL AS A CLEVER GUY WHO'S GOOD AT SPORTS. HE'S ALSO NORA'S MASTER. DESPITE SEEMING CALM AND COMPOSED, KAZUMA'S GOT QUITE A TEMPER. AS A RESULT, OTHER STUDENTS FEAR HIM. VERDICT: HE'S MORE DEVILISH THAN ANY DEMON.

NORA

THE DEMON WORLD'S PROBLEM CHILD, NORA'S FOUL TEMPER IS SURPASSED ONLY BY HIS STUPIDITY. NORA IS BETTER KNOWN AS THE VICIOUS DOG OF DISASTER, THE LEGENDARY DEMON CERBERUS. HIS POWER IS SAID TO SURPASS THAT OF THE DARK LIEGE HERSELF.

DARK LIEGE ARMY

HER INFERNAL MAJESTY, THE DARK LIEGE

THE COMMANDER-IN-CHIEF OF THE DARK LIEGE ARMY AND THE ONE WHO EXILED NORA TO THE HUMAN WORLD. WHEN SHE WEARS HER GLAMOUR SPELL, SHE'S ONE SMOKIN' HOTTIE. ALTHOUGH EVIL KEEPS HER BUSY, SHE NEVER NEGLECTS HER BEAUTY REGIMEN!

NAVAL FLEET GENERAL

RIVAN

LAID BACK AND SEEMINGLY LAZY, ONCE RIVAN SNAPS, NOBODY CAN HOLD HIM DOWN. HE'S INTO FISHING.

LAND CORPS GENERAL

LEONARD

THE DEMON WORLD'S NUMBER ONE GO-TO GUY. DEDICATED AND SERIOUS, LEONARD IS ALWAYS WORRYING, LEADING TO STRESS-RELATED MALADIES.

TENRYO ACADEMY MIDDLE SCHOOL, STUDENT COUNCIL

FUJIMOTO

KOYUKI HIRASAKA

THE BOSS

THE MYSTERIOUS HEAD OF THE RESISTANCE. RUMOR HAS IT HE KNOWS ALL THE SECRETS OF THE DEMON WORLD, BUT THERE'S ONE SECRET HE'S MANAGED TO KEEP TO HIMSELF: HIS TRUE IDENTITY.

KNELL

A MEMBER OF THE DEMON RESISTANCE WHO MAY HAVE HIS OWN SECRET AGENDA. OR MAYBE HE'D JUST RATHER PICK UP GIRLS. IGUNISU MAGIA HAS NO EFFECT ON HIM— INSTEAD, THE *LADIES* SEEM TO BE HIS WEAKNESS.

POOSON

HE'S FOUGHT AGAINST NORA IN THE PAST OVER A LITTLE MATTER OF JEWELRY. JEWELS CONTAINING THE DARK LIEGE'S SOUL, TO BE EXACT. HE USES A MAGIC CALLED "FUTURE READING" WHICH ALLOWS HIM TO GAUGE HIS OPPONENTS' MOVES AHEAD OF TIME.

KEINI

ALTHOUGH SHE SELDOM LEAPS INTO THE FRAY, KEINI'S A TERROR WHEN SHE'S MIFFED. SHE ALSO SEEMS TO HAVE A THING FOR HER BOSS.

LISTEN TO TEACHER! ♥

THE DARK LIEGE EXPLAINS IT ALL

HELLO, SWEETUMS, DARK LIEGE HERE.♥ MISS ME?

FOR THOSE WHO'VE JUST ARRIVED...GOSH, MY LITTLE DEMON PUP NORA HAS BEEN A BOTHER! DON'T I HAVE ENOUGH TROUBLE WITH THE RESISTANCE AND OUTLAW DEMONS REBELLING AGAINST MY DARK LIEGE ARMY WITHOUT NORA CAUSING ME PROBLEMS? THAT'S WHY I SENT MY STRAY DOGGIE TO THE HUMAN WORLD, TELLING HIM HE SIMPLY *MUST* LEARN TO BEHAVE.♥

OH, I'M SO WICKED! THE HUMAN I CHOSE TO HOUSEBREAK MY LITTLE CUR IS KAZUMA MAGARI.

BY ENTERING INTO A MASTER AND SERVANT CONTRACT WITH KAZUMA, NORA BECAME KAZUMA'S "FAMILIAR SPIRIT." AS SUCH, NORA CAN'T USE HIS MAGIC OR RELEASE HIS SEAL SPELL TO RETURN TO HIS REGULAR APPEARANCE WITHOUT HIS MASTER'S "APPROVAL."

MEANWHILE, THE BOSS OF THE RESISTANCE HAS SHOWN UP IN THE HUMAN WORLD. THAT BIG MEANIE SENT NORA'S POWERS EXPLODING OUT OF CONTROL, RELEASING MY PUPPY'S SEAL SPELL!! BOO! BUT NORA MANAGED TO SEAL HIS MAGICAL STREAM AGAIN...HOORAY! MY LITTLE PUP HAS GROWN SO MUCH...♥ KAZUMA FELT SIMPLY *TERRIBLE* THAT HE COULDN'T HELP NORA DURING THE BATTLE. NOW THAT NAUGHTY BOY'S GONE AWOL! I HEAR THAT HE'S "MATURING" SOMEWHERE. OH, I CANNOT *STAND* THE SUSPENSE!

CONTENTS

Story 17: Egomaniac

...!!
WHAT THE HECK'S GOING ON?

OW ...
UGH ...

OUR BUSINESS ASSOCIATES TOLD US THEY'D BEEN TRACKED BY THE DARK LIEGE ARMY, SO WE SHOWED UP HERE.
REDUCE SPEED
TENRYU THIRD TUNNEL
8.0 M
DO NOT ENTER
CAUTION
BUT THERE ARE DARK LIEGE ARMY SOLDIERS LYING AROUND HERE TOO, WHICH MEANS...
WAIT... YOU'RE A RESISTANCE MEMBER, RIGHT? I'VE NEVER SEEN YOUR FACE BEFORE.
WHICH UNIT DO YOU BELONG TO?

…
Story 17: Egomaniac

READ THIS WAY

WHO'S THE CREEPY GUY?
HE WAS ABLE TO BEAT THE DARK LIEGE ARMY ALL BY HIMSELF! HE MUST BE IN THE UPPER RANKS!
PSST
PSST
PSST
UH... THANKS!
THANKS FOR COLLECTING THE DARK LIEGE SOUL SHARDS...
S... SEE YOU LATER!
HEY, SOMETHING AIN'T RIGHT HERE! THE DARK LIEGE ARMY SOLDIERS ARE STILL ALIVE!!
JUST LEAVE IT TO MR. CREEPY. HE'LL DO THE CLEANUP WORK.
ALL WE NEED TO DO IS COLLECT THE DARK LIEGE SOUL SHARDS...
PSST
PSST
PSST
LET'S HURRY UP AND RETURN TO BASE!!
...

Unit
THE RESISTANCE HAS MANY UNITS AROUND THE HUMAN WORLD.
EACH UNIT HAS SEVERAL BASES, WHICH THEY UTILIZE AS NEEDED.
UOS
UNIT OF SATAN
HUH? WHAT'S THIS ABOUT UNITS?

IT'S SIMILAR TO THE WAY THE DARK LIEGE ARMY IS DIVIDED INTO THE FIRE, WATER, WIND AND LAND DIVISIONS.
EACH UNIT IS AFTER THE DARK LIEGE SOUL JEWELS, HOPING TO FIND THE REAL SOULS MIXED IN WITH THE OTHER STONES. THE UNITS ALSO CONTROL ACTIVITIES OF MEMBERS IN THE ASSIGNED REGION.

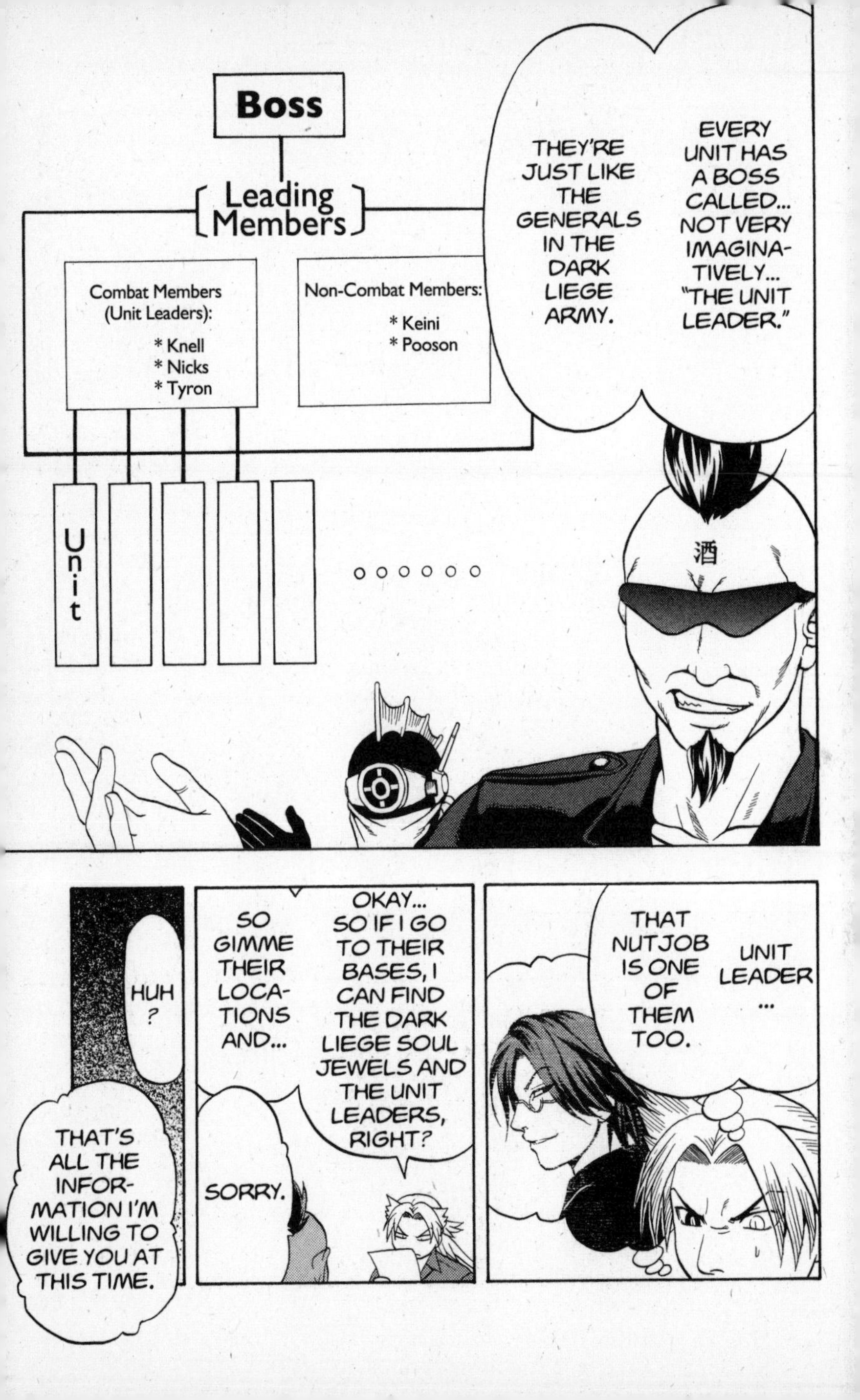
Boss
Leading Members
Combat Members (Unit Leaders):
* Knell
* Nicks
* Tyron
Non-Combat Members:
* Keini
* Pooson
Unit
EVERY UNIT HAS A BOSS CALLED... NOT VERY IMAGINATIVELY... "THE UNIT LEADER."
THEY'RE JUST LIKE THE GENERALS IN THE DARK LIEGE ARMY.
UNIT LEADER ...
THAT NUTJOB IS ONE OF THEM TOO.
OKAY... SO IF I GO TO THEIR BASES, I CAN FIND THE DARK LIEGE SOUL JEWELS AND THE UNIT LEADERS, RIGHT?
SO GIMME THEIR LOCATIONS AND...
SORRY.
HUH?
THAT'S ALL THE INFORMATION I'M WILLING TO GIVE YOU AT THIS TIME.

HEY, MAN! THAT'S A RIP-OFF! I HELD UP MY END OF THE BARGAIN.
YOU'RE NOT PLAYING FAIR!!
THOOM
YOU MADE ME BUY YOU ALL THOSE MUNCHIES !!
BOOZE AND JUNK FOOD ARE MY TWIN LOVES.
IT'S NOT LIKE THAT STUFF WAS HARD TO GET. I COULD'VE ASKED YOU FOR AN ARM OR A LEG.
YOU GOT OFF EASY, KID!
YO
IF ONLY IT WERE BASEBALL SEASON, I'D BE IN HEAVEN.
HERE, HAVE ONE.
I DON'T DRINK!
KLIK
YUCK!
I DON'T LIKE STUFF WITH BUBBLES!
IT BRINGS BACK BAD MEMORIES...
KLIK
TSHHH
!!!
HUMANS ARE AT THE TOP OF THE FOOD CHAIN BECAUSE WE CAN THINK AND USE TOOLS.

READ THIS WAY
...
BY THE WAY, MR. CERBERUS...
...YOU STRUCK OUT DURING THAT EXCHANGE AT THE TENRYO THIRD TUNNEL. I GAVE YOU THAT INFO, REMEMBER?
YEAH, SOME-THIN' CAME UP...
THAT GUY.
BY THE TIME I GOT THERE, NO ONE WAS AROUND.
THAT'S YOUR HARD LUCK. MY INFOR-MATION WAS SOUND.
LET ME TELL YOU SOME-THING ELSE YOU CAN USE.
THIS IS THE SECRET BASE OF THE UNIT THAT OVERSAW THAT EXCHANGE.
THE DARK LIEGE SOUL JEWELS YOU'RE LOOKING FOR SHOULD BE THERE.
!!
SO IF I GO THERE...
...I CAN FIND THE JEWELS AND THE UNIT LEADER!!

...IN SUMMARY, IF WE STRIKE A UNIT BASE, WE CAN CAPTURE THE UNIT LEADER.
IT'S ALL IN OUR RE-PORT.
YOU SHOULD LOOK THROUGH IT BEFORE I SEND IT IN.
I HATE DOING RESEARCH IN THE HUMAN WORLD. IT'S SUCH A HASSLE.
LOOK...
UOS

READ THIS WAY

...YOU WERE THE ONE WHO STARTED ALL THIS RESEARCH CRAP IN THE FIRST PLACE.
I'M COOL WITH THAT. THE RESISTANCE NEEDS LOOKING INTO.
BUT THE LEAST YOU CAN DO IS TO BE MORE RESPONSIBLE WHEN YOU'RE LOOKING AFTER SIR NORA.
RESPONSIBLE? I DON'T KNOW WHAT YOU'RE TALKING ABOUT.
SPLASH
PLOP
THINK IT OVER.
SHK
I KNOW WHAT THIS IS ABOUT. YOU DON'T KNOW IF IT'S SAFE FOR NORA TO STAY IN THE HUMAN WORLD.
YOU'RE SCARED OF WHAT HE MIGHT DO, AREN'T YOU?
IT'S TRUE THAT'S A PROBLEM... BUT I'M ON TOP OF IT.
LOOK, I KNOW YOUR POWER AND I'M AWARE OF HIS.
WHAT I DON'T KNOW IS WHY HE'S REFUSING TO COME BACK.
WHSH

NO!!
HE LASHED OUT AGAINST THE SUGGESTION THAT HE RETURN TO THE DEMON WORLD.
HE JUST SAYS NO WITHOUT GIVING ANY REASONS.
HIS SELFISHNESS IS A POTENTIAL RISK TO THE DARK LIEGE ARMY.
...
...
SELFISHNESS?
I'M NOT SO SURE. I THINK THAT MUTT'S **GROWN UP** A BIT.
HUH? HOW?
I CAN SEE IT NOW. THAT'S THE TARGET, RIGHT?
!
TUP

HOTEL CONOURA
SO THIS IS ONE OF THEIR BASES...
AN ABANDONED HOTEL?
HERE ARE OUR ORDERS. CAPTURE BUT DON'T KILL THE UNIT LEADER.
FSH
WE NEED TO INTERROGATE THE SUSPECT CONCERNING THE RESISTANCE.
BRINGING 'EM IN ALIVE IS SUCH A PAIN.
TAP
HEY, RIVAN!!
SLK
SLK

WHERE ARE THE DARK LIEGE SOUL STONES?
...
WHO IS THIS KID? WHERE'D HE COME FROM?
LOOK AT HIS STUPID CLOTHES. IS HE PRETENDING TO BE IN THE DARK LIEGE ARMY OR SOMETHING?
HIDEBU
阿部
UOS
WHAT? YOU GUYS ARE THE STUPID ONES!! LISTEN UP!
I'M CERBE...
SLAP
WHAT THE HELL ARE YOU DOING HERE?
HEY! WHAT'RE YOU DOING HERE?
AND WHY'D YOU GO AND SLAP ME?
...
SULK
HEY, MORE FREAKS ARE SHOWIN' UP.

HEY, I THINK I'VE SEEN THE TWO IN THE BACK SOMEWHERE BEFORE.
IF YOU GUYS'RE PART OF THE RESISTANCE, TELL US YOUR NAMES AND UNITS!
IF YOU CAN'T ANSWER BY THE COUNT OF THREE...
SOCKS
OUR UNITS?
WHAT'RE YOU LOSERS GONNA DO IF WE DON'T ANSWER?
WE'LL KILL YOU.
THREE ...
HERE'S YOUR ANSWER, PIG.

UOS
I'M NAVAL FLEET GENERAL RIVAN.
I BELONG TO THE DARK LIEGE ARMY.
UOS
WHAT THE ...?
THUD
HE'S GOTTA BE KIDDING!! THERE'S NO WAY A GENERAL WOULD SHOW UP **HERE**!!
WHO CARES? **KILL THEM**!!!

SWUP
SMASH
OW...
ZOOM
WHAM
SWIPE
AHH!
POW
DIE ALREADY, DAMMIT!!
THOK

THAT SWORD LOOKS LIKE A TOY!
MY MAGIC WEAPON'S GONNA SLICE IT TO BITS!!
SORRY.
I'M A PEACEFUL DEMON BY NATURE, BUT...
KLANG
GUH!
IT WON'T MOVE...
CRACK

KASHING
ZOOSH
YOU AND YOUR WEAPON ARE A PERFECT MATCH.
YOU'RE BOTH **ALL SHOW** AND **NO POWER**.

GET...
...OUTTA MY WAY!!!
LET THE BIG DOG HANDLE THIS ONE!!
POW
WHERE'S YOUR LEADER?
HAND OVER THE DARK LIEGE SOUL JEWELS!!!
HE FIGHTS LIKE A PUNK WITH A METAL BASEBALL BAT...
OH YEAH?
...
IT COMES FROM HANGING OUT WITH THE WRONG CROWD...
LIKE:
OR:
DON'T GET COCKY.

READ THIS WAY

THERE ARE PLENTY OF GUYS IN THE RESISTANCE WHO ARE WAY WORSE THAN US.
YOU GUYS WILL BE NO MATCH FOR THEM...
YOU SEEM TO KNOW A LOT.
WHERE'S THE UNIT LEADER AT THIS BASE?
WHERE ARE THE DARK LIEGE SOUL STONES?
YOU EXPECT A LOSER LIKE HIM TO KNOW THAT?
I CAN'T EVEN BOTHER TO LAUGH.

!!
CRASH

!!
U.O.S
UOS
HEY...
CHECK IT OUT!!

DARK LIEGE SOUL JEWELS!!!
HEY, MAN, HAND OVER THOSE JEWELS!!
WUP
!!
WHOOSH
THAT THE UNIT LEADER?
MUST BE. YOU CAN JUST SENSE THAT HE'S NOT LIKE THE OTHER GOONS.
BUT WHAT'S WITH THAT...
...MASK?

HANG ON, SIR NORA.
WE HAVE TO CAPTURE HIM, NOT KILL HIM.
NO!!
DAK
ANOTHER REQUEST REFUSED.
PLEASE STOP THIS POINT-LESS GRAND-STAND-ING...
IT'S NOT POINT-LESS!!
I SAID I WAS GONNA FIGHT, SO SHUT UP AND WATCH!!
...SO HE SAYS.
WANT TO LET HIM GO?
...
ALL I CAN SAY IS I'M NOT TAKING RESPON-SIBILITY...
...FOR WHATEVER HAPPENS NEXT.

MAN, THIS DUDE'S CREEPY.
...THE WIND SOUL STONE!!
THAT'S ... !!
POP
WHOOSH
HEY!! HOW COME YOU'VE GOT...

CLANG
HUH?
!!
HE BLOCKED ME WITH HIS BARE ARM!
SLAM
WHOA !!
POW

UGH...
WHAT'S UP WITH THAT ARM?
FWMP
IT'S COVERED IN A MAGICAL STREAM!
HE'S ABOUT TO FORM A MAGICAL WEAPON.
HE'S MAKING THE STREAM TANGI-BLE.
WE HAD SOMEONE LIKE THAT IN THE DARK LIEGE ARMY... SOMEBODY WHO WAS GOOD AT THAT SORT OF THING.
IT TAKES A LOT OF MAGIC POWER TO FEND OFF SIR NORA'S MAGIC WEAPON.
IF THIS GUY MANAGES TO CREATE A MAGIC WEAPON, WE'RE IN BIG TROUBLE.
SIR NORA ISN'T READY FOR AN OPPONENT LIKE THIS.

THIS GUY'S GOOD!!!

TZING

WHOOSH
KICK

POW
OOF !!

IT'S NOT LIKE HE'S ALL THAT FAST.
EVEN THOUGH HE'S NOT USING MAGIC, HE CAN READ MY MOVES AHEAD OF TIME!!
SKREE
IT'S LIKE HE CAN PREDICT EVERY MOVE I'M GONNA MAKE!!
BUT THAT'S NOT THE MOST ANNOY-ING PART...
GRR GRR

HOW DARE YOU FIGHT ME WITH JUST ONE ARM?
IS YOUR OTHER HAND BUSY WITH SOME-THIN'?
SWUK
GAH
POW
GAH!
THAT COCKY BASTARD ...
STILL HOLDING BACK, HUH? DON'T UNDER-ESTIMATE ME!!!

I'M GONNA MAKE YOU USE BOTH ARMS!!
"I DECLARE" IGUNISU MAGIA: BLACK FLAME WINGS!!!
UOS
UNIT OF SATAN
...
CRAP!! I CAN'T DO THAT WITHOUT KAZUMA'S APPROVAL!!
POW

HE HASN'T BROUGHT OUT A FINISHING MOVE OR A MAGICAL WEAPON... HE'S TOYING WITH SIR NORA.
'FRAID SO. OUR PUP'S IN FOR A **LONG, SLOW** BEAT-ING.
POW
POW
SIR NORA! YOU CAN'T EVEN STAND UP NOW!
PLEASE RETREAT!
I... ALREADY SAID NO...
OUR GOAL IS TO OBTAIN THE DARK LIEGE SOUL STONES!
DON'T GET DISTRACT-ED FROM THE MISSION!!
GRR
NO!!
THIS IS SELFISH AND POINT-LESS...
NO!! THERE'S A POINT!!
I HAVE TO LEARN TO FIGHT ON MY OWN!

THERE'S NO POINT IF I CAN'T WIN!!
KLIK
MR. CERBER-US, PLEASE TELL ME ONE THING.
Beer
IF YOU OBTAIN ALL THE PIECES OF THE DARK LIEGE'S SOUL, WHAT ARE YOU GOING TO DO WITH THEM?
WHAT? I'M GONNA KILL MS. UGLY, OF COURSE!
I SEE... SO YOUR GOAL IS TO ELIMINATE THE DARK LIEGE.
酒
YOU'RE JUST LIKE THE BOSS OF THE RESISTANCE.
Beer
...
UOS

I JUST WANT TO BE STRONG.
HER UGLY MAJESTY IS SUPPOSED TO BE AS STRONG AS THEY GET.
THAT'S THE REASON I WANNA DEFEAT HER.
I DO THAT, AND I'LL NEVER LOSE TO ANYBODY AGAIN!!
UOS
UOS
I DON'T WANNA BE A SLAVE TO MY MAGIC POWER.
I DON'T WANNA GET **USED** BY A NUT LIKE KAZUMA.
AND I WANT TO SHOW THE OTHER GUYS MY STRENGTH!!

I'M SMARTER THAN ANYONE THINKS!!
WHEN I WAS LOCKED UP...
...I DIDN'T KNOW ANYTHING.
IT'S ALL BECAUSE OF KAZUMA!!
HE DRAGGED ME AROUND AGAINST MY WILL...
...BUT I LEARNED A LOT FIGHTING WITH HIM!
TH OK
I LEARNED THINGS ABOUT MYSELF I DIDN'T WANT TO KNOW!!

GRP
LIKE HOW MUCH I WANNA BE STRONG! HOW I NEVER WANNA LOSE AGAIN!
I DIDN'T WANNA KNOW THAT I WANTED IT THAT BAD!!
...
FINE, BUT IT DOES SEEM SELFISH.
MAYBE SIR NORA HAS CHANGED A BIT...
SO IT'S NOT POINT-LESS, EH?
...BUT HE'S STILL A STUPID PUPPY.
DID YOU KNOW THAT ABOUT YOUR-SELF?
COME ON!!
DAMN IT!
I'M GUESSING HE DOES NOW.
WHAT ARE WE GOING TO DO ABOUT THIS?
POW POW

NO MATTER WHAT... I'M GONNA MAKE THIS ASSHOLE USE BOTH ARMS!!
HE'S FOCUSING ALL HIS ENERGY ON THE STREAM.
IF I CAN MAKE HIM LOSE FOCUS, THE STREAM WILL DISSOLVE!!
THERE'S GOTTA BE A WAY.
EVEN A **HUMAN** CAN FIGHT AGAINST A DEMON IF HE USES HIS SMARTS.
HUMANS ARE AT THE TOP OF THE FOOD CHAIN BECAUSE WE CAN THINK AND USE TOOLS.
...
GRP

THERE !!
FWASH
HE THREW A CHUNK OF CON-CRETE!
WHAT THE HECK IS HE DOING?
IS HE TRYING TO USE IT AS A SHIELD?
SNEAK
THAT GUY WILL BLAST RIGHT THROUGH IT!!
SHEESH !!
HERE I AM COPYING THAT HUMAN IDIOT!
BOOM

THANKS FOR NOTHIN', KAZUMA!!
A BEER CAN?

HE THREW THEM BOTH AT ONCE!
THE CAN WAS BEHIND THE CON-CRETE!!
IT DISRUPT-ED THE STREAM!!
SWIP

!!
A MAGIC WEAPON!!
...!

CRASH
WOW!
HEH...
TAKE THAT, CREEP-SHOW!!
...
I MADE YOU USE BOTH HANDS AND YOUR MAGIC WEAPON!!
BWA HA HA!!
MAN, I FEEL WAY BETTER NOW!!
OKAY, LET'S START OVER, AND THIS TIME I'LL WASTE YOU!!
HEH...
HEH HEH...
HUH?
...?
HA HA HA...

ZOOSH
KASHIN
DRAT!
TZZT
SIR NICKS!
GEEZ, I STEP AWAY FOR A MINUTE AND EVERYTHING GOES TO HELL! WHAT'S GOING ON HERE?

WHY ARE THESE DEMONS HERE?
THE NAVAL FLEET GENERAL, THE LAND CORPS GENERAL, CERBER-US...
HUH?
WHO'S THAT GUY IN THE BLACK COAT?
HMM...
HE'S NOT ONE OF THE LEADERS OF THE RESIS-TANCE..
THAT GUY WITH THE WINGS WAS AT THE PORT.
HE'S GOT NERVE...
AQUA MAGIA...
...DOUBLE DRAGON WATER WAVE!!!
VOOSH
OOPS...
THAT DIDN'T QUITE WORK.

BOOM
YOW!
RETREAT, SIR NORA!!
WHOA ...
I'VE GOTTA GET OUTTA THIS!!!
"I DECLARE" IGUNISU MAGIA, BLACK FLAME WINGS...
WAIT, I CAN'T DO THAT WITHOUT ...

"I APPROVE."

OOM

HEH... YOU SHOULD SEE THE LOOK ON YOUR FACE.
WHAT A RUSH.
AH... WHA...
WHAT'S THE MATTER? ARE YOU SUCH A STUPID MUTT YOU'VE FORGOTTEN ABOUT ME AFTER ONLY TWO MONTHS?
IN THAT CASE, ALLOW ME TO INTRO-DUCE MYSELF.

MY NAME IS KAZUMA... KAZUMA MAGARI.

I HOLD YOUR CONTRACT. I'M YOUR MASTER, STRAY DOG.

Story 18: The Need for Power

TO DEAL WITH ME, THE CLIENT SACRIFICED FIVE YEARS OF HIS LIFE.
Story 18: The Need for Power

FIVE YEARS?
YOU'RE FIVE YEARS OLDER?
HE'S TALLER THAN ME... JUST LIKE THE REST...
DRIDE
GRM GRM GRM
NO...
?
CHK
THIS CAN'T BE JUST FIVE YEARS' DIFFERENCE!!
He's how old now?
Now he's three years older than me!!
YOU'RE SO TALL!! YOU LOOK SO MATURE!! THIS CAN'T BE HAPPENING!
GAAH
HEH
HUH?

"I FORBID."
GAKK!
ARGH... IT'S KAZUMA, ALL RIGHT.
I RECOGNIZE THIS SADISM!!
HEH HEH...
DID YOU SHRINK? YOU'RE LIKE A MINIATURE POODLE.
SNAP
KRRK
GRP
SAY THAT AGAIN, PUNY HUMAN!

DASH
OH, HELLO, PAIN.
SWIK
YEESH ...
...
BARKING AGAIN, MY LITTLE PUPPY?
GAH!!
JAB
BONK

CRASH
...
YOU HAVEN'T CHANGED. YOU STILL SUCK!!
AND YOU STILL DON'T KNOW YOUR PLACE. YOU'RE A MUTT WITH-OUT AN OUNCE OF BREEDING.

READ THIS WAY
I'M NOT A MUTT!!
WHAT THE HECK IS GOING ON?
THAT GUY KAZUMA DEALT WITH IS A DEMON WHO USES TIME MAGIC. I'VE HEARD OF HIM BEFORE.
I THOUGHT HIS TYPE ONLY GAVE OUT INFOR-MATION.
MAYBE HE GAVE KAZUMA THE KNOWLEDGE TO PERFORM THE MAGIC HIMSELF.
BUT A HUMAN BEING CAN'T HAVE THAT MUCH CONTROL OVER THE MAGICAL STREAM, NOT EVEN THE MASTER OF CEREBUS ...
HANG ON. REMEMBER WHO KNOWS ABOUT THAT KIND OF HIGH-LEVEL TECHNIQUE?
!
PLINK
OH NO, NOT...

ZZING
I DON'T CALL **THIS** A WARM WELCOME.
AREN'T YOU HAPPY TO SEE ME?
YOU CURSED SCUM.
BE GLAD I DECIDED TO GO EASY ON YOU.
WELL, WELL, WHAT A SUR-PRISE.
HEY!

IT'S BEEN A WHILE, RIVAN AND LEONARD.
YOU'VE GROWN UP, SIR NORA... BUT YOU HAVEN'T **GROWN SMART**.

MELFIA?
THAT'S MY TEACHER.
FIRE BRIGADE GENERAL MELFIA...
YOU WERE AWAY ON A SPECIAL MISSION.
WHAT'RE YOU DOING HERE?
WHY THE HELL DIDN'T YOU CONTACT US?
I MADE A LITTLE BOO-BOO.
WHILE YOU'VE BEEN GONE I'VE HAD TO PICK UP YOUR SLACK...
...WHICH I HAD TO PICK UP FROM HIM...
I KNOW YOU CAN HEAR ME!!

READ THIS WAY

SIR NORA.
WHAT?
I'VE HEARD A LOT ABOUT YOU FROM YOUR BUDDY.
WHILE I WAS GONE YOU POLISHED YOUR SKILLS IN IGUNISU MAGIA, RIGHT?
DAMN STRAIGHT.
BUT NOT JUST FIRE-TYPE MAGIC ...
SOUNDS PROMIS-ING. I'D LOVE TO SEE IT.
HOPE IT'S NOT TOO MUCH FOR YOU...
...CUZ I'M GONNA SHOW YOU RIGHT NOW!!
NO, I'M SURE YOU'RE TIRED.
I'D RATHER SEE YOU AT THE HEIGHT OF YOUR POWERS.
HEY, NO WAY!
OKAY, I'VE GOT NO CHOICE BUT TO...

HOLD IT!
NOTICE HOW SHE CHANGED THE SUBJECT? GUESS SHE DOESN'T FEEL LIKE GIVING US AN EXPLAN-ATION.
SHE ALWAYS HAD HIM WRAPPED AROUND HER LITTLE FINGER.
AFTER ALL THIS TIME, YOU'RE STILL A FOOL.
WHAT'D YOU SAY?
SORRY. I MEANT YOU'RE STILL A SIMPLE-MINDED, EASILY MANIP-ULATED FOOL.
FIVE YEARS OLDER AND HE'S STILL A JERK.
AND HE STILL KNOWS HOW TO GET UP MY ASS.
NOW THEN...
OH NO!! HERE COMES THE CHOKE COLLAR...
TU P
HEY... WHERE'RE YOU GOING?
WE FOUND THE BASE OF ANOTHER RESIS-TANCE UNIT NEARBY.

THANKS TO THIS DARK LIEGE SOUL STONE, I WAS ABLE TO LEARN QUITE A LOT.
OH YEAH!! WHERE'D YOU GET THAT?
...HEY, WAIT UP!!
TUP
WHAT'S UP WITH HIM? WHY DOESN'T HE DRAG ME AWAY BY FORCE LIKE HE USED TO?
WHAT THE HELL IS HE UP TO?
...
ARE YOU REALLY RESPONSIBLE FOR KAZUMA'S MASTERY OF THE STREAM?
Wait for me!!
YEAH, IT WAS ALL ARRANGED THROUGH THAT INFORMATION BROKER.
I ACCEPTED THE DEAL BECAUSE THE IDEA... INTRIGUED ME.
I MADE AN EX POST FACTO REPORT TO THE DARK LIEGE JUST NOW.

SO...
...HOW'D YOU DO IT?
EVEN IF KAZUMA IS THE CONTRACT HOLDER OF CERBERUS' MAGICAL POWER, HE'S STILL ONLY HUMAN.
HOW DID YOU TEACH A HUMAN BEING TO CONTROL THE STREAM?
I JUST CARRIED OUT STANDARD STREAM CONTROL TRAINING.
EVEN BEFORE I BEGAN TO TEACH HIM, MAGICAL POWER HAD ALREADY BEGUN TO PERMEATE HIS BODY.
BUT WHY?
FUNNY, ISN'T IT?
HE WAS QUITE THE UNIQUE CHALLENGE...
...AND FAR MORE **INTERESTING** THAN I'D EXPECTED.
UOS

FWOOSH
MEOWWW!!
WRONG. DON'T DODGE THE FLAME.
FWUMF
CONCENTRATE THE STREAM ONTO YOUR ARM AND **CATCH** IT.
DUCK AGAIN AND I'LL KILL YOU.
P... PLEASE WAIT!!
MEOW... HOW'D A SCAREDY-CAT LIKE ME GET SUCKED INTO A SITUATION LIKE THIS?
Oops, my hand slipped.
Where am I going now?

I'LL JUST BE OVER HERE!!
DON'T WANT TO GET IN THE WAY OF THE TRAINING!!
YOU STAY RIGHT THERE.
WHAT? WHY?
THIS IS A LESSON IN FIGHTING WHILE PROTECTING A PARTNER.
KAZUMA HAS TO LEARN TO FIGHT AS PART OF A PAIR.
...
GRP
MEOW!
DON'T GET THE WRONG IDEA!
TOSS
MEOW!!!

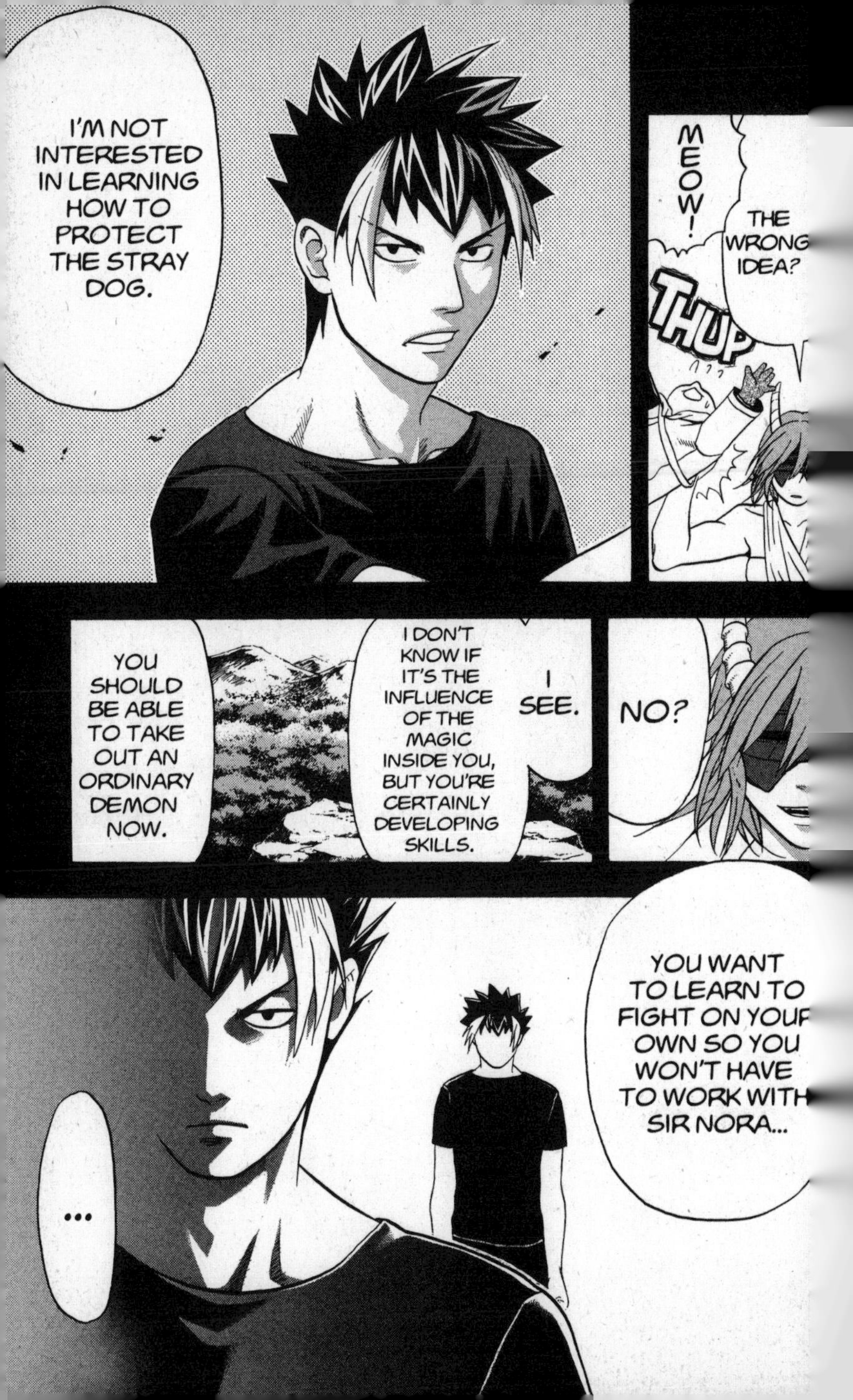
THE WRONG IDEA?
MEOW!
THUP
I'M NOT INTERESTED IN LEARNING HOW TO PROTECT THE STRAY DOG.
NO?
I SEE.
I DON'T KNOW IF IT'S THE INFLUENCE OF THE MAGIC INSIDE YOU, BUT YOU'RE CERTAINLY DEVELOPING SKILLS.
YOU SHOULD BE ABLE TO TAKE OUT AN ORDINARY DEMON NOW.
YOU WANT TO LEARN TO FIGHT ON YOUR OWN SO YOU WON'T HAVE TO WORK WITH SIR NORA...
...

HEY, WAIT!!
C'MON, HAND IT OVER!!
THE DARK LIEGE SOUL STONE?
IF THAT'S WHAT YOU WANT, YOU CAN HAVE IT.
THUP
I GOT THAT CHUNK OF SOUL AND THE CERBERUS MASK FROM MELFIA.
...
TUP
TUP
SHE GOT THEM FROM SOMEONE ELSE, BUT I DON'T KNOW WHOM.
I WAS AT THE BASE TRACKING THE DARK LIEGE SOUL GEMS.
I HANDED A CASE OF FAKES TO THE OUTLAW DEMONS SO I COULD FIND OUT HOW THEY WERE DISTRIB-UTED.
TURNS OUT THIS ONE WAS REAL. GOOD THING I MARKED IT JUST IN CASE.
He vandalized a piece of my soul?

...
GEEZ ...
WHAT'S BOTHERING YOU, NORA?
I'M THE ONE WHO STILL NEEDS TO COLLECT INFORMATION.
THAT'S NOT IT!
YOU'RE ACTING WEIRD EVEN FOR YOU. WHAT'RE YOU PLOTTING?
WHY'RE YOU BEING ALL HONEST AND NONVIOLENT?
CHK
THERE'S NO NEED FOR THAT SORT OF THING ANYMORE, IS THERE?
HUH?

WHO THE HELL ARE THOSE DEMONS?
THEY'RE UP TO NO GOOD!!
THEY MIGHT BE THE GUYS WHO ATTACKED THE BASE NEARBY...
LET'S KILL 'EM!!
WHY NOT?
CRAP... MORE DISTRAC-TIONS.
SHF SHF
HEY!! BEHIND YOU!

!!

KILL... THEM...
BAD IDEA...
TZI
NG

TZI
NG

SMASH
KEEP GETTING IN THE WAY AND I'LL CRUSH YOU ALL.
...

WHAT'S UP WITH HIM?
THERE'S NO WAY HE'S STRONGER THAN ME!
BUT HE'S TOUGHER THAN MOST DEMONS!!
GRP
NOT BAD FOR A HUMAN!!
'COURSE, HE COULDN'T DO IT IF HE WASN'T USING MY MAGIC POWER!!
...
GRR GRR GRR GRR

WHOA...
WHAT'S GOING ON?
WHY IS THIS GETTING ME SO PISSED OFF?
UOS
UOS

ZSH
GAH!!
CHOMP
YOU...
YOU SEEM DISTRACT-ED, STRAY DOG.
I REFUSE TO LET YOU GET IN MY WAY.
SNAP
...!!

YOU'RE STILL JUST A STUPID HUMAN!!
WOOSH
DON'T YOU UNDER-STAND THE SITU-ATION YET?
CLANG
I DON'T HAVE TIME TO DEAL WITH YOU!
GETTING ALL HIGH AND MIGHTY AGAIN? DON'T UNDER-ESTIMATE ME!
WE'LL SETTLE THIS HERE, ONCE AND FOR ALL!!
WHY ARE YOU SO IRRITATED?

LOOK, THIS CAN WAIT UNTIL WE GET RID OF THESE GUYS...
NO IT CAN'T !!
!!
THAT'S ENOUGH!
WAK
HEY!
I TOLD YOU TO NOT GET IN MY WAY!! I CAN PROTECT MYSELF!
SLASH
THUD
I'M IN YOUR WAY? MAN, YOU'VE GOTTA BE JOKING.
...!!
I MEAN...
YOU MEAN TO SAY BEING PROTECTED BY ME IS A JOKE?

NO WONDER PEOPLE THINK YOU'RE DUMB.
?!
DON'T GET THE WRONG IDEA!
I'M NOT INTERESTED IN LEARNING HOW TO PROTECT THE STRAY DOG.
NO? I SEE.
YOU WANT TO LEARN TO FIGHT ON YOUR OWN SO YOU WON'T HAVE TO WORK WITH SIR NORA.
...
WRONG ON ALL COUNTS, LADY.

I'M SAYING THAT HE NO LONGER NEEDS ANY PROTECTION FROM ME. HE'S STRONGER THAN BEFORE.
WHOOSH
WHY DO YOU THINK I AGREED TO SHAVE THOSE YEARS OFF MY LIFE?
I DON'T WANT THE POWER TO PROTECT HIM OR THE POWER TO FIGHT ON MY OWN.

WHAT I WANT IS THE POWER TO BE HIS EQUAL.
WIPE THAT DUMB LOOK OFF YOUR FACE. DON'T YOU GET IT YET?
DID YOUR BRAIN TURN TO JELLY WHILE I WAS GONE?
KILL THEM !!
...

I THOUGHT YOU'D GOTTEN SMART ENOUGH TO LOOK AFTER YOURSELF. I SUPPOSE I WAS WRONG.
IT LOOKS LIKE YOU STILL NEED MORE EDUCATION.
I'LL HAVE TO EDUCATE YOU WITH EXTREME PRE-JUDICE...
...SO BE PRE-PARED!
USE MAGIC, STRAY DOG!!
WE'LL WIPE THEM ALL OUT AT ONCE!!
UOS
HMPH...
...?

WHERE DO YOU GET OFF LORDING IT OVER ME?
YOU'RE STILL RELYING ON MY POWER!!
I DON'T LIKE IT, BUT DON'T FORGET YOU'RE **USELESS** SOLO!!
I HAVE NO CHOICE. THIS IS A SPECIAL CASE...
"I DECLARE" ANEMOSU MAGIA, HEAVY THUNDER FLASH!
...
HEH HEH ...
I SEE... SO THAT'S IT.
HUH?

I THOUGHT THERE WAS SOME SERIOUS ISSUE AT STAKE...
...BUT YOU'RE JUST POUTING BECAUSE YOU FEEL NEGLECTED.
WHY... YOU...
YOU'RE UPSET BECAUSE YOU THINK IF I BECOME STRONGER...
...I WON'T NEED YOU ANYMORE.
HEHHEH HEHHEH
...!!
ARGH!
SNAP SNAP
NO!! THAT'S NOT IT!!
OH YES IT IS.
WOULD YOU LISTEN TO ME? THAT'S NOT IT AT ALL! GET IN MY FACE AGAIN AND I'LL **KILL**—
"I APPROVE."
...

I'LL KILL YOU, HU-MAN!!!
I'D LIKE TO SEE YOU TRY, DOG.

BOO

WIND
SPIRIT
FIRE
WATER
EARTH
THE FIRE SOUL STONE IS HELD BY SIR NORA, AND THE WATER SOUL STONE IS HELD BY THE RESISTANCE.
I HAVE A PRETTY GOOD IDEA OF WHO HOLDS THE EARTH SOUL STONE.
I HAD THE WIND SOUL STONE, BUT I GAVE IT TO NORA'S MASTER.
G... GAVE IT?
WHY WOULD YOU DO THAT, MELFIA?
BE-CAUSE HE IN-TRIGUED ME.
I THOUGHT YOU WERE MORE CALCU-LATING THAN THAT.
IT **IS** A CALCU-LATION, LEONARD.
I'M SURE HE'LL MAKE GOOD USE OF IT.
I JUST CAN'T SAY EXACTLY **HOW**...

DAMMIT... JUST LIKE I THOUGHT, YOU'RE STILL NOTHIN' BUT TROUBLE.
WHAT ARE YOU DIGGING FOR? ARE YOU GOING TO BURY A BONE?
DIG DIG
DIG DIG
Huh? Bone?
I'M LOOKING FOR A DARK LIEGE SOUL STONE!
IT MIGHT BE BURIED AT THIS BASE!!
IT'S NOT HERE.
HUH? HOW DO YOU KNOW?
WHAT A PATHETIC SCENE.
AND AFTER I CAME ALL THIS WAY ON A MATTER OF BUSINESS.
SHK
HEY! YOU'RE...

...THAT SWINDLER, POOSON!!
WHAT'RE YOU DOING HERE?
ALL RIGHT, LET'S GET DOWN TO BUSINESS, PENCIL-PUSHER.
HUH ?
WHUP
THUP
I'M A SERIOUS BUSINESSMAN, CONTRACT-HOLDER!
!!
THOSE ARE...
...THE FIRE SOUL STONE AND THE WIND SOUL STONE!

WHEN DID YOU ...?
NO, WAIT... **WHY** DID YOU GIVE THEM TO **HIM**?
HMMM...
THAT IDIOT'S TOO DUMB TO PUT ON AN ACT.
THESE MUST BE **REAL**.
WHAT?
THERE THEY ARE, JUST AS PROM-ISED.
TIME FOR OUR **EX-CHANGE**.
WE WANT YOU TO GUIDE US TO HIM.
GIVE US THE LOCATION OF THE MASTER-MIND IN THE MASK.
UOS UNIT OF SATAN

THESE ARE MY ROUGH SKETCHES OF KAZUMA AFTER GROWING UP A BIT. PEOPLE WROTE TO ASK ABOUT HIS NEW HEIGHT. ANSWER: 190 CM (ABOUT 6'2"). KAZUMA IS AS TALL AS HIS FATHER SHINICHIRO.

VROOOM
GRR
GRR
GRR
...!!
WHAT NOW, STRAY DOG?
GRR GRR
CALM DOWN.
HOW AM I SUPPOSED TO DO THAT?
DON'T YOU UNDERSTAND WHAT YOU'VE GOTTEN US INTO?
Story 19: The Discharge
ZUZUGI

OF COURSE. WE'RE RIDING A RESISTANCE VEHICLE INTO THE BOSS'S HEAD-QUARTERS.
THIS IS THE QUICKEST WAY.
DO YOU HAVE A PROBLEM WITH THAT?
Though I think they chose this mode of transportation just to annoy us...
I'VE GOT A CRAPLOAD OF PROBLEMS!! YOU GAVE THEM OUR DARK LIEGE SOUL STONES!
HEY!!
BETTER WATCH YOUR BACK, CON ARTIST!
WHEN WE GET THERE, I'M GONNA KILL YOU AND TAKE BACK THE DARK LIEGE SOUL STONES!!
MAN, BIG TALK!
YOU CERTAINLY ARE A HOT-HEAD, DEMON.
I STILL THINK THIS IS A BAD IDEA, MR. POOSON.
ARRANGING THIS EXCHANGE ON YOUR OWN AND BRINGING THEM TO MEET THE BOSS...
HA! THERE'S NO NEED TO WORRY! I HAVE NO INTENTION OF LETTING THEM SEE THE BOSS!!
THE RESIS-TANCE WILL TERMINATE THEM BEFORE THEY GET TWO STEPS IN.

FWASH
WHAT MATTERS IS THAT I'M HOLDING BOTH THE FIRE SOUL STONE AND THE WIND SOUL STONE!
AS LONG AS I HAVE THESE, I'M ON THE FAST TRACK TO A PROMOTION !!
I SHOULD'VE KNOWN YOU HAD A PLAN, MR. POOSON !!
YOU KEEP SAYING THIS'LL BE QUICK...BUT SINCE WHEN HAVE YOU BEEN INTO KICKING ASS? DIDN'T THINK YOU CARED ABOUT FIGHTING.
WHAT?
I GET THAT YOU GOT STRONGER SO YOU WOULDN'T BE TOTALLY USELESS IN BATTLE.
BUT WHAT MADE YOU GO THIS FAR?
...
IT'S BEYOND YOUR DOGGIE BRAIN.
I'M NOT A... GEEZ, NEVER MIND!
HUH? WHAT'S THAT?
A GUY STAND-ING IN THE MIDDLE OF THE ROAD...
HEH... I'LL JUST RUN HIM OVER.
VROOM
OH...
WAIT, THAT'S...

...KNËLL!
GOOD EVENING, FRIENDS... ♪
FWUM
IT'S HIM!!
JUMP, DOG!!

BOOM
YOW !!

WH... WHAT ARE YOU...
THUD
UGH...
Tink
Tink
THUD
OOH ...
THAT RAT BAS-TARD!!

I SEE!
YOU ...
SWUK
WOW!
YOU USE THE STREAM TO PROTECT YOUR ARM, RIGHT?
THAT'S A PRETTY INTERESTING TECHNIQUE, KAZUMA.
IT'S SUPPOSEDLY IMPOSSIBLE FOR MAGICAL POWER TO PENETRATE A HUMAN BODY IN THE FIRST PLACE...
HEY !!

I STOPPED BY AFTER HEARING THE NEWS FROM NICKS. LOOKS LIKE THINGS ARE STARTING TO GET INTERESTING AGAIN.
AND I GOT TWO DARK LIEGE SOUL STONES IN THE BARGAIN!
HEY, GIVE THOSE BACK!!
BUT SACRIFICING PART OF YOUR LIFE TO GAIN POWER... THAT'S REALLY HARD-CORE.
I COULD SEE SELLING OFF A COUPLE OF YEARS WHEN YOU'RE OLD AND GREY...
...BUT I'D REFUSE TO GIVE UP MY YOUTH. THOSE ARE KEY YEARS FOR A PLAYER LIKE ME!
...
I CAN'T IMAGINE YOU'LL **EVER** STOP FOOLING AROUND.
SHOWS WHAT YOU KNOW.
WHEN I WAS YOUR AGE, I HAD A TOTALLY UPTIGHT JOB, AS THEY SAY.
"UPTIGHT JOB"?

DARK LIEGE ARMY LIEUTENANT GENERAL.
TZZT
RIVAN?
TP
!
ON TOP OF THAT, HE'S A TRAITOR ...
WHAT'RE YOU DOING HERE?

HELLO, GENERAL RIVAN. WORRIED ABOUT YOUR PET PUPPY?
OH, BUT I WON'T DO ANYTHING LIKE I DID **LAST TIME.** WHY NOT JUST LET ME GET AWAY AGAIN?
HUH? WHAT'S HE TALKING AB...
...
YEARS AGO, WHEN I LEARNED HE WAS A TRAITOR...
...I WAS THE ONE RESPONSIBLE FOR LETTING HIM ESCAPE.
!
I WON'T LET YOU GET AWAY THIS TIME.
WE'L SETTLE THIS **ONCE AND FOR ALL.**

WHAT'S THE BIG IDEA?
OOPS, I THOUGHT YOU WERE GOING FOR A SURPRISE ATTACK.
YOU'RE NO PUSHOVER, HUH? GUESS THE FOUR GENERALS ARE AS TOUGH AS THEY SAY.
LOOK, YOU...
SHOOF
THE NAME'S KNELL.
YOU PROBABLY DON'T REMEMBER ME. I BECAME A LIEUTENANT GENERAL OF THE FIRE BRIGADE JUST THE OTHER DAY.
Restricted Area
No Fishing!!

A LITTLE NIGHT FISHING?
I DIDN'T THINK I'D RUN INTO ANYONE IN THIS RESTRICTED AREA.
...
THIS IS A PROBLEM.
IF YOU HADN'T STUMBLED BY, I COULD'VE DEALT QUIETLY WITH THE DOG OF DISASTER.
ZZZ
SAKE CHIPS
UNIT OF SATAN
ARE YOU AFTER THE POWER OF CERBERUS?
YOU'RE TRESPASSING ON THE PROPERTY OF THE DARK LIEGE ARMY. EVEN IF YOU CAN SHAKE ME OFF, YOU WON'T GET AWAY.
HA HA... DON'T WORRY 'BOUT THAT. ♪

I KILLED ALL THE GUYS WHO WERE ON PATROL.
AND SINCE I CAN MAKE DEAD DEMONS INTO FAMILIAR SPIRITS...
THEY TRUSTED ME...WHICH MADE THEM EASY PREY.
...I SENT THEM TO BUY ME A LITTLE MORE TIME.
UOS

...
THE PROBLEM IS HOW TO SHAKE YOU OFF... ♪
KRIK
YOU...
KRIK
OH? IS IT OKAY TO USE MAGIC?
A TOUGH GUY LIKE YOU CAN BLOW AWAY THE SCENERY WITH A WAVE OF YOUR HAND.
JUST BE CAREFUL NOT TO LOSE YOUR CUTE LITTLE PUPPY...
!!

ANG
SO THAT'S THE DEAL?
SKREE
SKREE
'CAUSE OF ME, YOU LOST YOUR CON-CENTRATION AND LET HIM GET AWAY?
BUT WHY...
...
BACK THEN YOU WERE EVEN **MORE** OF A FOOLISH BRAT THAN YOU ARE TODAY.
HEY...

BECAUSE OF THAT OUR HANDS WERE TIED.

WE COULDN'T LET YOU DIE WHILE YOU WERE STILL YOUNG AND NAÏVE...
...BACK WHEN YOU STILL DIDN'T KNOW WHAT YOU WANTED TO BE WHEN YOU GREW UP.
HA HA... ARE YOU KIDDING? WAS HE LIKE A LITTLE BROTHER TO YOU?
HOW ABSURD COMING FROM A SOLDIER...
GRR
IS THAT COMPASSION I HEAR? SINCE WHEN DO DEMONS ACT SO PATHETICALLY HUMAN?
WE'RE NOT A PROTECTIVE SPECIES. DEMONS USE PEOPLE.
JUST KEEP TALKING, SCUM...
DAK
YOU'RE NOT GOING TO USE MAGIC?
THIS TIME YOU DON'T NEED TO HOLD BACK.

I SAID I WAS GOING TO SETTLE THIS.
I'LL DEAL YOU WITH THE SAME WAY I DID THAT TIME...
ZOOP
GRUP
YOUR WEAKNESS IS THAT YOU HAVE NO ATTENTION SPAN... ♪

!!!
THAT !! GUY...
JEEK?
I THOUGHT HE WAS DEAD...
THAT'S RIGHT. THAT'S HOW HE BECAME MY FAMILIAR SPIRIT.

!!
GAH!
RIVAN !!
BLOOP
ZOOSH
YOW !!
SWIK

TAP
YOU HAVE THE GREATEST ATTACK POWER OF THE FOUR GENERALS.
Pretty dangerous...
BUT MY ATTACK JUST NOW WAS PRETTY EFFECTIVE TOO, HUH?
THAT'S DIRTY POOL! YOU HAD A FAMILIAR SPIRIT UP YOUR SLEEVE!
FIGHT FAIR AND SQUARE!!
FAIR AND SQUARE? HA HA... DON'T BE SILLY.
DA
DEMONS NEVER FIGHT FAIR.
BOOM
HATRED, FEAR, GREED...
LEGEND HAS IT THAT WE WERE BORN FROM THE DARKEST HUMAN EMOTIONS.
BEFORE YOU KNEW IT, WE STARTED **LOOKING** LIKE HUMANS. WE BUILT OUR OWN SOCIETY AND PASSED EASILY BETWEEN THE HUMAN AND DEMON WORLDS.

WHONG
DEMONS WEREN'T MEANT TO LIVE IN HARMONY WITH HUMANS.
THAT'S BORING. THAT'S WHY WE HAVE TO BE REBORN.
WE STARTED TO LOSE OUR DEMONIC IDENTITIES, POWERS AND GOALS.
GAH!
HE'S A FORCE OF DISASTER THAT CAN LEVEL THE DEMON WORLD AND HUMAN WORLD ALIKE.
THAT'S WHY WE NEED CERBERUS.
...
UOS

OUT OF THE RUINS WILL COME HORRIBLE PEOPLE WITH TERRIBLE, DARK MOTIVATIONS.
AND FROM THEIR MINDS DEMONS WILL RISE AGAIN, MORE POWERFUL THAN EVER...
HEH HEH HEH...
THAT'S NOT JUST CRAZY. IT'S STUPID TOO.
YOU INSANE CLOWN.
WE DEMONS ARE THE ULTIMATE.
YOU'RE JUST HUMAN.
KLANG

!!!
ZSH
!!!
DON'T GET IN MY WAY. THIS IS MY PROB-LEM...
IT'S MY PROB-LEM TOO!!
HE JUST WANTS TO USE ME IN HIS CRAZY PLANS!
KLANG
IT PISSES ME OFF TO THINK OF HIM SITTIN' BACK AND LAUGHING AT ME!!
!
I DON'T WANNA OWE YOU EVEN MORE THAN I ALREADY DO 'CAUSE OF THIS LOSER!

THAT'S WHY THIS IS MY PROBLEM...
...AND I'M GONNA SETTLE IT HERE AND NOW!!
...
KNELL AND NORA... AND I... HAVE A HISTORY.
KICKING HIS ASS MIGHT BE A GREAT WAY TO TEST OUR POWERS.
HA HA! YOU GUYS ARE A TAG TEAM NOW?
YOU SURE ARE COCKY NOW THAT YOUR BOY-FRIEND'S BACK, NORA!
DON'T UNDER-ESTIMATE ME!!
SWUK
ON THE CON-TRARY. YOU UNDER-ESTIMATE ME.

IGUNISU MAGIA: SCORCHING TORNADO!!!
UGH!
TZZT
DAMN IT! "I DECLARE" IGUNISU MAGIA...
DON'T DO IT. FIRE DOESN'T WORK AGAINST HIM.
THEN "I DECLARE" AQUA...
...
TZZT
CAN IT BE THAT...
...YOU TWO HAVE...

...GOTTEN BORING?
SH
ARGH!
I THOUGHT WITH THE RETURN OF KAZUMA YOU'D GO THROUGH SOME DRAMATIC CHANGE!
OW!
UOS
YOU HAVEN'T CHANGED AT ALL. PATHET-IC.
THIS MUST BE THE LIMIT OF YOUR POWER WHEN THE CONTRACT HOLDER IS A HUMAN...
FWUMP

SLASH
YOUR POWERS AS THE HOUND OF HADES ARE BEING UTTERLY WASTED.
WHAT A SHAME. MAYBE YOU TWO SHOULD JUST DIE NOW...
...
IS IT TRUE THAT I'M HOLDING YOU BACK, STRAY DOG?
HUH? ARE YOU AGREEING I CAN'T BRING IT?
IGUNISU MAGIA: BURNING BLACK DRAGON ...
VWOOSHH

MAYBE IT'S TRUE.
LOOK, YOU WERE BORN TO BECOME THE STRONGEST DEMON EVER. MAYBE IT'S MY FAULT THAT YOU'RE NOT.
AS YOUR MASTER, I SHOULD HAVE HELPED YOU DEVELOP. INSTEAD I GOT IN THE WAY.
KRIK
KRIK

KRAK
KRAK
ROARR
NUTS ...
THAT FIRE DRAGON'S GOING TO BE POWERFUL ...
THE FIRST TIME I SAW YOU...
...I KNEW YOU WERE JUST THE CHANGE I NEEDED IN MY LIFE.
YOU GAVE ME A PUR-POSE.
HAVING THE WORLD'S MOST POWER-FUL DEMON AS MY FAMILIAR SPIRIT...

I WAS DETER-MINED TO MAKE YOU THE STRONGEST OF THEM ALL!
BDMP

I GAVE UP FIVE YEARS OF MY LIFE SO I COULD BE A TRUE PARTNER TO YOU. SO I COULD HELP YOU REALLY FIND YOURSELF.
THUP
BDMP
I DID IT BECAUSE I WANTED TO BE WORTHY OF BEING YOUR MASTER.
I CAN'T JUST QUIT HELPING YOU BECOME STRONGER.
I'VE GOT TO MAKE IT HAPPEN.
BDMP

IT'LL MAKE ME PROUD TO SEE YOU TAKE YOUR PLACE AS THE STRONGEST DEMON EVER.

THE STREAM...

WHAT AN INCRED-IBLE WAVE OF MAGICAL POWER!
I DON'T KNOW WHAT YOU'RE PLANNING TO DO, BUT IT'S TOO LATE!
I'M GOING TO KILL YOU!!
ROAR
...
"I APPROVE."

BURNING BLACK DRAGON!!!

WHAT THE HELL? IS THIS THE SAME MAGIC?
HOW WAS HE ABLE TO ACTIVATE IT SO QUICKLY?
DON'T FORGET, I WAS BORN WITH A TOLERANCE FOR FIRE-TYPE MAGIC.
NO MATTER HOW STRONG THE MAGIC IS, IT WON'T AFFECT...
CHOMP
WHA...

AAAAA...
AAAA...
AAAAAAH!
I'M HOT...
THIS IS IMPOSSIBLE!!
I'M BURNING!
I'M SUPPOSED TO BE IMMUNE!
THIS CAN'T BE HAPPENING...

!!
ACK...
UGH...
SHLK
SPCH
THUD

GR
P
VOOP
WHY ARE YOU STOPPING ME? ONE MORE BLOW AND IT'S OVER!
YOU'RE NOT SHOWING MERCY, ARE YOU?
...
HOW'S IT FEEL TO LOSE TO YOUR OWN GREATEST STRENGTH?
I IMAGINE THE DEMON WORLD WILL SEE YOU AS A REAL LOSER.
...
SHUT UP AND KILL ME, HUMAN!
NO.

I WON'T KILL YOU. THAT'D BE LETTING YOU OFF THE HOOK.
I WANT YOU TO LIVE WITH YOUR TOTAL AND COMPLETE HUMILI-ATION.
I WANT YOU TO WATCH, HELPLESS, AS THE BLEAK FUTURE YOU WORKED SO HARD FOR IS DESTROYED.
...
WHOOSH
I'LL MAKE YOU REGRET THIS...
I'LL QUENCH THE FIRE OF THIS SHAME...
SHAAAAA

...WITH YOUR BLOOD!
THE EMBLEM OF CERBERUS APPEARED BEFORE THE SEAL SPELL WAS RELEASED.
...
FIRST MAGICAL POWER PERMEATED A HUMAN BODY. THEN NORA SOMEHOW GOT SOME BRAINS...
IT'S JUST ONE IMPOSSIBLE THING AFTER ANOTHER.
WHAT THE HELL IS HAPPEN-ING?
AND WHY IS IT HAPPENING TO THEM?

Story 20: Destiny

AIEEE!!
KNELL LOST!
KNELL, WHO WAS AS STRONG AS ANY GENERAL IN THE DARK LIEGE ARMY...
THAT STUPID MUTT NORA TOLD ME NOT TO UNDER-ESTIMATE THEM. BUT THAT'S EXACTLY WHAT I DID.
CREEP
LOOKS LIKE THE MARKET'S CRASHED ON THE RESIS-TANCE!!
CHOK
YIPE!!

Story 20: Destiny
THANKS FOR WAITING, PENCIL-PUSHER.
NOW, IF YOU DON'T WANT TO DIE, I SUGGEST YOU TAKE US TO THE **MASTER-MIND.**
IT WAS SUPPOSED TO BE A BUSINESS DEAL.
NOW IT'S MORE LIKE A **HOSTILE TAKEOVER** !!!

...
UOS
UOS

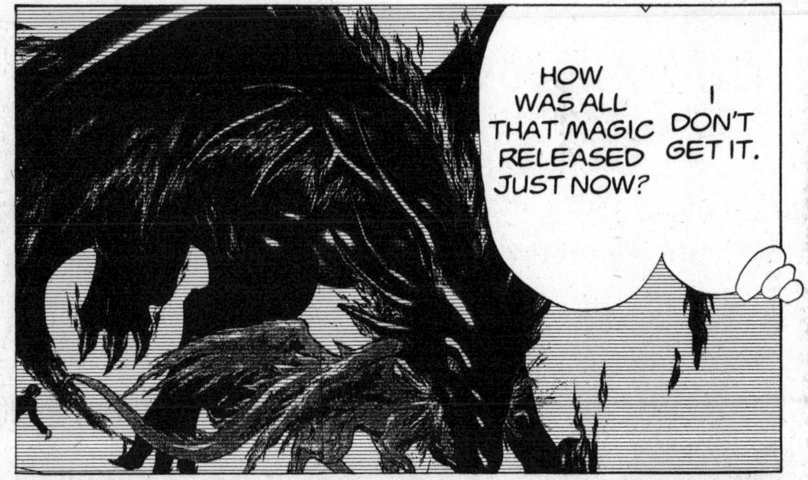
I DON'T GET IT.
HOW WAS ALL THAT MAGIC RELEASED JUST NOW?

IT'LL MAKE ME PROUD TO SEE YOU TAKE YOUR PLACE AS THE STRONGEST DEMON EVER
THE SLEEPING DOG THAT WAS DORMANT INSIDE ME...
HAS IT REALLY AWAKENED? WILL IT REALLY MAKE ME STRONG?
BDMP
BDMP

HEY, WHAT DO YOU THINK...
RIVAN?
WHERE THE HECK DID HE GO?
...
WELL, THAT WAS CERTAINLY IMPRESSIVE.
VMMM
YOU GOT HURT BECAUSE YOU TRIED TO FIGHT WITH YOUR MAGICAL POWER RESTRAINED. YOU'RE NOT USED TO IT.
THE METHODS YOU'VE USED IN THE PAST WON'T WORK THE SAME WAY NOW.
YOU KNOW, YOU COULD LEARN A HEALING SPELL OR TWO. I'M TIRED OF BEING YOUR NURSE-MAID.
BLAH
BLAH
BLAH
BLAH
UGH... GIVE IT UP, YOU OLD GOAT.
I'D RATHER BLEED OUT THAN LISTEN TO YOU BITCH AND MOAN.
THIS ISN'T JUST A FLESH WOUND. SHUT UP AND LET ME HELP YOU.
I'm not old...
THE GREATER THE OPPONENT'S POWER, THE MORE DIFFICULT THE WOUND IS TO TREAT.
TUP
WE'LL RETURN TO THE DEMON WORLD FOR THE TIME BEING.
SHK
HUH?
YOU'RE GOING TO PRETEND YOU DIDN'T SEE WHAT JUST HAP-PENED?

TUP
WHAT?
DIDN'T YOU SEE IT? THAT HUGE DISCHARGE OF MAGIC!
AND THAT EMBLEM APPEARING ON SIR NORA'S FOREHEAD...
IF SIR NORA KEEPS GROWING, WILL KAZUMA BE ABLE TO CONTROL HIM?
DIDN'T YOU FEEL JUST A LITTLE... SCARED?
I MEAN, SIR NORA **IS** THE HOUND OF HADES, AFTER ALL...
...
WHOOSH

DEMON WORLD
AW! PREZZIES FOR LI'L ME! ♡
AND ALL MY FAVES! MY GOODNESS!!
MELFIA, YOU'RE SUCH A SWEETIE-PIE!!
I'M TICKLED PINK! ☆
TEE HEE!
I LIKE TO THINK I KNOW THE DARK LIEGE'S TASTES.
I ONLY WISH I COULD GAZE STRAIGHT INTO YOUR SOUL...
YOU SWEET-TALKER... ♡
TEE-HEE...

READ THIS WAY
I'M GOING OUT FOR A WHILE. SEE THAT MY GUEST IS WELL TREATED. ♡
TOK
YES, MA'AM.
I'LL LEAVE THE REST TO YOU, KAIN.
CHAK
...
SHE'S A BUSY WOMAN.
SO MANY PRIVATE, SECRET AFFAIRS... SHE'S QUITE THE ENIGMA.
PUTTING SIR NORA UNDER CONTRACT SEEMED TO BE SOMETHING OF A WHIM...
...BUT PERHAPS...
...
TUP
HOW'S YOUR INJURED HAND DOING?
IT APPEARS IT WAS DIFFICULT TO TREAT... QUITE UNUSUAL.
GOVERNOR-GENERAL AIDE KAIN.

STRANGE THINGS ARE HAPPENING TO BOTH THE CONTRACT HOLDER AND SIR NORA.
UNUSUAL CHANGES THAT CAN'T BE EXPLAINED AWAY...
...
I DIDN'T DEAL WITH SIR NORA VERY MUCH IN THE PAST.
What does a friend of ol' Ugly want with me?
UOS
BACK THEN HE WAS JUST A YAPPING PUP. YOU COULDN'T EVEN GLIMPSE THE LEGENDARY HOUND OF HADES BENEATH THE SURFACE.
BUT NOW...
...HE'S A FORCE TO BE RECKONED WITH.

HOW MUCH FARTHER ARE YOU GONNA MAKE US WALK?
ARR RGH
ARE WE THERE YET?

LOOK AT THIS MIST.
IT'S ODD. THE TEMPER-ATURE AND AIR QUALITY SEEM WRONG...
YUP.
IT'S BECAUSE WE'RE ALREADY PAST THE EN-TRANCE !!
WHAT ?
THERE ARE SEVERAL ENTRANCES TO THE DEMON WORLD THAT ONLY KEY RESISTANCE MEMBERS KNOW HOW TO USE.
TAK

WHAT DO YOU MEAN?
YOU'RE IN ENEMY TERRI-TORY.
YOU'D BETTER WATCH YOUR STEP.

ENEMY ...?
WHOOSH

THIS IS THE DEMON WORLD.

THIS IS THE HEAD-QUARTERS OF THE RESISTANCE.

THIS IS... ...THE DEMON WORLD?
...
UOS
IT'S TRUE THAT IT DOESN'T LOOK LIKE THE HUMAN WORLD...
I MEAN, FIVE SUNS?
I SEE.
SINCE YOU HAVE SO MANY BASES IN THE HUMAN WORLD, ONE MIGHT ASSUME THAT YOUR HEADQUARTERS WOULD ALSO BE THERE.
THAT'S WHAT THE DARK LIEGE ARMY PROBABLY THOUGHT.
THEY COULDN'T SEE THE FOREST FOR THE TREES.
MOST LIKELY THE RESISTANCE PUT UP A BARRIER TO KEEP THEM OUT.
...

THE DEMON WORLD'S SKY...
EVEN WHEN I WANTED TO, I REALLY COULDN'T SEE IT VERY WELL...
...
UOS
HUH?
HEY!!
THAT SWINDLER'S GONE!!
HE DIDN'T STEAL THE DARK LIEGE SOUL STONES, DID HE?
THEY'RE RIGHT HERE.
...!!!
YOU'RE COLLECTING ALL FIVE, RIGHT?
I'LL LOOK AFTER THEM UNTIL THEN.
MELFIA TOLD ME THAT THE MASTERMIND HOLDS THE WATER SOUL STONE.
!!
UOS

I FOUND IT...
THE SPIRIT SOUL STONE...
THE MOST IMPORTANT DARK LIEGE SOUL FRAGMENT OF ALL...

MY NAME'S NORA!!

WHAT'S YOUR NAME?

HEY!
DAHLIA!!
Oh!
POP
TIME TO EAT!!
YOU COULD AT LEAST TALK TO ME!!
LOVE ME MORE
KEINI...
YOU'RE STILL TRYING TO PICK THE REAL DARK LIEGE SOUL SHARDS OUT OF THE FAKES?
SEEMS KINDA DUMB TO ME.
EVEN THOUGH YOU CAME HERE AGAINST YOUR WILL, YOU WORK SO HARD.
I WONDER WHY THE BOSS WANTS THE DARK LIEGE SOUL STONES ANYWAY.
THE DEMON HOUND IS AFTER THEM TOO, RIGHT?

I HEARD FROM NICKS THAT HIS GANG JUST BROKE INTO THIS AREA.
THEY'RE PROBABLY LOOKING FOR THE DARK LIEGE SOUL STONES. TALK ABOUT STUBBORN!!
...!
I... I'M SORRY ...
VMM
HUH?
TERA MAGIA: CRADLE OF THE LAND!!!
SHF
!!
KRICH

ER...
...SORRY ABOUT THAT.
NORA'S HERE!!
HFF
HFF
HEY, WHY CAN'T YOU PLAY WITH ME ANY-MORE?
HFF
HFF
I WANT TO PLAY WITH YOU, I SWEAR. BUT SIR KAIN WILL SCOLD ME IF HE FINDS OUT...
I'M NOT AFRAID OF THAT GUY!!

HE SAYS YOU'RE SPECIAL IN SOME WAY.
THAT'S WHY I'M SUPPOSED TO STAY AWAY FROM YOU...
...
HOW AM I THE ONLY ONE WHO'S SPECIAL? WE'RE BOTH FROM ANCIENT RACES, RIGHT?
I HATE BEING SPECIAL.
OH!
HMPH! GUESS THEY'RE JUST AFRAID OF ME!
I AM THE MOST POWERFUL DEMON, AFTER ALL!!
THAT WASN'T EXACTLY IT.
MAYBE NOW HE'D UNDERSTAND WHY HE HAD TO BE ISOLATED.
HFF
PLEASE, NORA...
PLEASE STOP TRYING TO BECOME STRONGER...
HFF

I DON'T LIKE THE LOOK OF THIS PLACE.
IT LOOKS JUST LIKE THE RESTRICTED AREA BACK WHEN I WAS A KID.
SHK
ARE YOU TALKING ABOUT ...
... THE DARK LIEGE ARMY FACILITY WHERE YOU WERE ISOLATED ALONG WITH OTHER MEMBERS OF THE ANCIENT RACES?
SHK
HUH. NOT "ALONG WITH."
THE OTHER KIDS WERE FORBIDDEN TO GO NEAR ME.
THEY WERE JUST SUPPOSED TO HANG AROUND UNTIL I GREW UP.
UOS
...?
WHY? WHAT PURPOSE DID THEY SERVE?
BEATS ME!
I WAS JUST TOLD THEY WERE NECESSARY FOR ME TO BECOME A MATURE CERBERUS...
A MATURE CERBERUS ...

WHOOSH
YOU'RE A FOOL, CERBERUS.
TUP
THAT VOICE!!
IT'S DANGER-OUS FOR YOU TO BE HERE.

FWOOSH
DON'T YOU FEAR DEATH?

SO THE BIG BOSS SHOWS UP PERSONALLY TO GREET US.
YOU ...
LAST TIME WE MET, YOU MADE A FOOL OUTTA ME!
HAND OVER THOSE DARK LIEGE SOULS!!!
WHY DO YOU CONTINUE TO PURSUE THE DARK LIEGE SOUL FRAGMENTS?
HUH? TO FIGHT THE DARK LIEGE!! DUH!
I'M GONNA BEAT THE DARK LIEGE AND PROVE I'M THE STRONGEST!!
THE **STRONGEST?** IN WHAT WAY?

WSH
IN EVERY WAY! MAGIC!! MARTIAL ARTS!! I'M GONNA BE STRONGER THAN ANYBODY ELSE!
EVERYBODY'S GONNA SEE THAT I'M THE BIG DOG!!
WSSH
I DON'T THINK IT'S THAT SIMPLE...
...BUT IT'S GOOD TO HAVE A GOAL.
...
YOU DON'T UNDER-STAND THE IMPLI-CATIONS...
...OF CERBERUS GROWING INTO THE MOST POWERFUL DEMON.
...?
IT'S NOT TOO LATE...
SHHP

HE'S COMING!!
CHK
PLEASE WAIT!!
STOP...
PLEASE STOP!!
!!
HUH?
DAHLIA?
IS THAT REALLY YOU?
YOU KNOW HER?

SHE USED TO BE IN THE RESTRICTED AREA LIKE ME.
WHAT'S SHE DOING HERE?
SHK
SHK SHK
THIS ISN'T WHAT YOU PROMISED ME.
YOU SAID YOU WOULDN'T KILL NORA!!
YOU SAID YOU'D MAKE HIM UNDERSTAND!!
?!
AFFAIRS ARE MOVING FASTER THAN I EXPECTED.
IF I LET THIS CONTINUE, IT'LL BE TOO LATE.

TO STOP IT, I WILL **GLADLY** KILL THESE TWO.
BR
BR

UOS

BOOM
KOFF ...
NNGH !!
THUD
CLINK
CLINK

HEY...
WHOOSH
!!
NORA, RUN AWAY!
ARGH...
EVEN WITH THE MAGICAL POWER OF CERBERUS, YOU CAN'T DEFLECT MY ATTACKS.
IN THE END, YOU'RE JUST A PUNY HUMAN.
YOU FOOLISHLY TRIED TO GAIN POWER THROUGH CERBERUS. THAT WAS ARROGANT OF YOU.

YOU'LL SOON REGRET THAT MISTAKE.
YOUR MINDLESS PURSUIT OF POWER JUST BOUGHT YOU DEATH.

READ THIS WAY

IT'S STILL NOT TOO LATE.
IF THE CHOSEN ONE DIES NOW, THE MASTER AND SERVANT CONTRACT WILL BE DISSOLVED.
YOUR MAGICAL POWER WILL RETURN TO YOU, NORA!!
!!
THERE'S NO REASON YOU CAN'T ESCAPE TO THE OUTSIDE WORLD.
THE DARK LIEGE ARMY ISN'T HERE TO HOLD YOU BACK.
YOUR FREEDOM AWAITS YOU!!

FREE-DOM...
BDMP
BDMP
REMOVE THE CON-TRACT, HUMAN PUNK...
...OR I'LL EAT YOUR SO-
YOU GOOD-FOR-NOTHING LOWER CLASS ANIMAL.
IF HE DIES...
...I'LL BE FREE, BUT...

READ THIS WAY

HEH HEH ...
MINDLESS PURSUIT OF POWER, EH?
I WON'T DENY IT.
IF YOU THINK MY ONLY MOTIVE IS IDLE CURIOSITY, THAT'S FINE BY ME.
GRP
IT'S NOT ENTIRELY FALSE.
I'M RISKING MY LIFE BECAUSE I HAVE AN INTEREST IN DOING SO. PLUS IT'S FUN. WHAT'S WRONG WITH THAT?
BDMP
IF HE DIES...
...WHAT WILL I DO WITH MY FREE-DOM?
BDMP

WILL I ...
... BE-COME THE STRONG-EST?
IN THE PAST ...
...I HEARD SIMILAR WORDS FROM ANOTHER FOOL.
WSSH
YOU TWO SEEM BOUND TO SHARE THE SAME FATE.
VMM
VMM

THIS BLADE...
...WILL SEVER THOSE CHAINS OF FATE.

SO YOU STILL HAVE SOME STRENGTH.
BUT IT'S USELESS. MY BLADE CAN SLICE THROUGH ANYTHING.
TZING
FLESH, CERTAINLY, BUT ALSO...
KRIK

KRAK
NNG!
...IT CAN EVEN CUT THROUGH A SOUL...
CHOK

UNGH
...
UOS

NORA...

...I...
...WANT TO BECOME THE STRONG-EST...
PEOPLE ALWAYS TOLD ME I HAD TO... TO BE RESPECT-ED...
...BUT ALL THEY REALLY WANTED WAS TO CONTROL MY POWER... TO LIMIT IT... TO CONTROL AND LIMIT ME.
BEFORE THIS JERK CAME ALONG, NOT A SINGLE PERSON REALLY WANTED ME TO BE STRONG!!
THOSE DEMONS WERE ALL AFRAID... JUST 'CAUSE SOME STUPID LEGEND...
ptui
...
...SAYS THE HOUND OF HADES IS GONNA DESTROY THE DEMON WORLD AND HUMAN WORLD...
THIS CREEP ...
GRP

...IS THE ONLY GUY WHO REALLY WANTS TO HELP ME GET STRONGER!!!
IT'LL MAKE ME PROUD TO SEE YOU TAKE YOUR PLACE AS THE STRONGEST DEMON EVER.
IT DOESN'T MATTER WHY HE CARES... AS LONG AS HE DOES.
IT'S FINE BY ME!!
I'M GONNA MAKE IT HAPPEN...
I DON'T NEED TO BE FREE TO DO THAT!!
I'LL USE HIM TO BECOME THE STRONG-EST!!
I WAS DETERMINED TO MAKE YOU THE STRONGEST OF THEM ALL.

UNTIL HE DOES, I'LL PROTECT HIM FROM LOSERS LIKE YOU!!
UOS

...
HOW FOOL-ISH.
BUT THAT SORT OF DETER-MINATION CAN'T BE SLICED IN TWO, EVEN WITH THE BLADE OF EXTINC-TION.
...?
THEN IT'S NO LONGER SIMPLY A PROBLEM OF KILLING YOUR MASTER.
I GUESS I'LL HAVE TO TELL YOU THE SAD TRUTH.
SHK
KARMA'S A BITCH, CERBERUS.
SLUKK
BE CAREFUL WHAT YOU WISH FOR.
CARE-FUL?
YES.

TRY TO BECOME THE STRONGEST... AND YOU'LL DIE.

HUH?

GRA
DIE?
NO WAY!!
AIEE!!
IT'D BE JUST AS IF THE DARK LIEGE KILLED YOU HERSELF.
DESTRUCTION IS YOUR FATE, CERBERUS.
HUH? WHAT'RE YOU TALKING ABOUT?
ARE YOU SAYING THE DARK LIEGE WANTS TO KILL ME?
...
PERHAPS. IF YOU WANT TO LEARN THE REASON, CLIMB THIS WALL.
SHK
HEY! WAIT !!
GRRM
WHOA !!
SHK

GET BACK HERE AND EXPLAIN YOURSELF!!
WHAT DO YOU MEAN BY...
DAMMIT!
DESTRUCTION IS MY FATE?

Volume 5: Destiny—End

CHARACTER DATA

MELFIA

HEIGHT: 176 CM
FAVORITE FOOD: FINGER SANDWICHES
LEAST FAVORITE FOOD: KAHLUA AND MILK
INTERESTS AND SPECIAL TALENTS: READING (ESPECIALLY HISTORICAL BOOKS AND DICTIONARIES)
NOTES: THE GENERAL OF THE FIRE BRIGADE AND AN EXCELLENT TEACHER. BECAUSE OF HER APPEARANCE AND JOB, PEOPLE TEND TO ASSUME SHE'S JUST A THUG, BUT SHE'S ALSO WELL READ AND AN EXCELLENT STRATEGIST. HER TRAINING REGIMEN IS SAID TO BE INTENSE.

DAHLIA

HEIGHT: 153 CM
FAVORITE FOOD: MINERAL WATER
EAST FAVORITE FOOD: SPICY FOODS
INTERESTS AND SPECIAL TALENTS: GARDENING, FLOWER ARRANGEMENT
NOTES: A DEMONESS FROM ONE OF THE ANCIENT RACES WHO GREW UP IN THE SPECIAL CLASS AREA LIKE NORA. SHE WAS NORA'S SECRET PLAYMATE WHEN THEY WERE KIDS.

ROUGH CHARACTER SKETCHES I DREW BEFORE I STARTED *NORA.*

GROOMER, PART 1
HEY! THERE'S SOME-THING I WANT TO ASK.
ACHOO
IS IT TRUE THERE'S A REALLY STRONG HUMAN...
...CALLED "GROOM-ER"?
I HEAR THIS GUY'S SECRET POWER IS "GROOMING." IT CHANGES THE VICTIM'S APPEARANCE LIKE MAGIC!
NO MATTER HOW BIG AND STRONG THE OPPONENT IS, HE OR SHE CRIES LIKE A BABY AFTER BEING "GROOMED"!
ER... WHO DID YOU HEAR THAT FROM?
THAT CREEP.
I KNEW IT...
ACHOO
GROOMER, PART 2
ACTUALLY, MY JOHNNY IS FINE WITH GROOM-ING!
REALLY?
YEAH! NOT ONLY DOESN'T HE RESIST IT, HE SEEMS TO LIKE IT.
HE ISN'T BOTHERED BY ANY-THING THE GROOMER DOES.
JOHN HIRASAKA
Nora's Imagination
IT SEEMS THERE'S AN INCRED-IBLY BRAVE DUDE NAMED JOHN AT THE VICE-PRESI-DENT'S PLACE!
I KINDA WANT TO SEE HOW HE LOOKS AFTER BEING "GROOMED."
YEAH. HIS COAT USED TO BE A REAL MESS, JUST LIKE YOURS ....

BOOKSTORE OF HORRORS
THIS IS A TRUE STORY...
MY FAMILY RUNS A SMALL BOOKSTORE. I WORK THERE PART-TIME.
ONE DAY A COLD RAIN WAS FALLING AND THERE WEREN'T MANY CUSTOMERS.
I WAS PREPARING TO CLOSE THE STORE.
SUDDENLY I SENSED THAT SOMEONE WAS STANDING AT THE BACK OF THE STORE.
THE DOOR WAS RIGHT BEHIND ME AND IT WAS LOCKED.
WHEN I'D LOOKED AROUND A FEW MINUTES BEFORE I HADN'T SEEN ANYONE.
Beep beep
Beep beep
HE LOOKED LIKE A DEMON.
WHAT IS IT, LEONARD? DON'T HASSLE ME...
LOOK, YOU OLD GOAT, STEP OFF. I MEAN IT, BALDY...
WHAT? YOU'RE NOT BALDING?
THEN I'LL **MAKE** YOU BALD, DAMMIT... I'LL PULL IT ALL OUT...
WHAT DID YOU JUST SAY? HEY! STAY RIGHT THERE!
WITH THOSE WORDS, THE STRANGER VANISHED INTO THIN AIR.
TZZT
Fish
?!
HE'D BEEN READING A FISHING MAGAZINE. CREEPY, HUH?
...
ACHOO

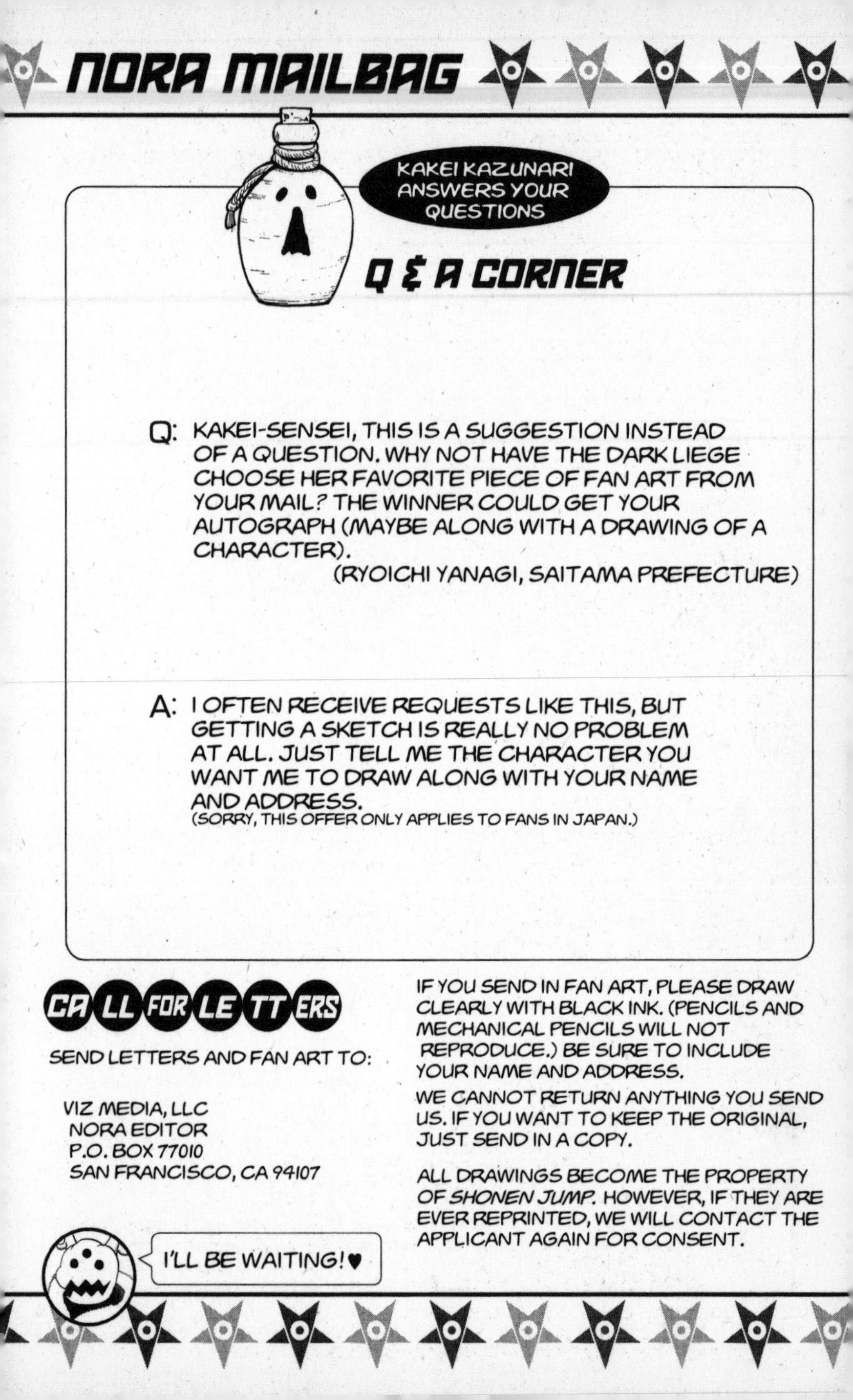

NORA MAILBAG
KAKEI KAZUNARI ANSWERS YOUR QUESTIONS
Q & A CORNER
Q: KAKEI-SENSEI, THIS IS A SUGGESTION INSTEAD OF A QUESTION. WHY NOT HAVE THE DARK LIEGE CHOOSE HER FAVORITE PIECE OF FAN ART FROM YOUR MAIL? THE WINNER COULD GET YOUR AUTOGRAPH (MAYBE ALONG WITH A DRAWING OF A CHARACTER).
(RYOICHI YANAGI, SAITAMA PREFECTURE)
A: I OFTEN RECEIVE REQUESTS LIKE THIS, BUT GETTING A SKETCH IS REALLY NO PROBLEM AT ALL. JUST TELL ME THE CHARACTER YOU WANT ME TO DRAW ALONG WITH YOUR NAME AND ADDRESS.
(SORRY, THIS OFFER ONLY APPLIES TO FANS IN JAPAN.)
CALL FOR LETTERS
SEND LETTERS AND FAN ART TO:
VIZ MEDIA, LLC
NORA EDITOR
P.O. BOX 77010
SAN FRANCISCO, CA 94107
IF YOU SEND IN FAN ART, PLEASE DRAW CLEARLY WITH BLACK INK. (PENCILS AND MECHANICAL PENCILS WILL NOT REPRODUCE.) BE SURE TO INCLUDE YOUR NAME AND ADDRESS.
WE CANNOT RETURN ANYTHING YOU SEND US. IF YOU WANT TO KEEP THE ORIGINAL, JUST SEND IN A COPY.
ALL DRAWINGS BECOME THE PROPERTY OF SHONEN JUMP. HOWEVER, IF THEY ARE EVER REPRINTED, WE WILL CONTACT THE APPLICANT AGAIN FOR CONSENT.
I'LL BE WAITING! ♥

OUR DEVILISH STAFF PAGE
THE FIENDISH STAFF THAT PARTICIPATED IN VOLUME 5 (IN NO PARTICULAR ORDER)
THREE ASSISTANTS WORK IN THE STUDIO PER DAY. THEY CHANGE EVERY DAY. THERE ARE TIMES WHEN THERE ISN'T A BALANCE BETWEEN THE NUMBER OF PEOPLE WHO SAY GOOFY THINGS AND THE NUMBER OF PEOPLE WHO FIRE OFF SNARKY COMEBACKS.
Listen to Teacher!
OKAY...
AT LEAST WE GET THE HOLIDAYS OFF!
SMELLS LIKE FISH!
...
OKAY...
THERE SURE ARE LOTS OF TAXIS WAITING...
GOOFY
GOOFY
GOOFY
MAJIN GYO!
...
I'VE FORGOTTEN WHAT ONE LOOKS LIKE!!
A DAY OFF?
A BUTTERFLY!! COOL!!
PLEASE, SOMEBODY COME OVER!!
I'M SO SORRY!
Empress Yoshinon
HER SHARP TONGUE IS A DEADLY WEAPON.
Chef Hitouji
BRILLIANT ILLUSTRATOR AND COOK.
Ohga-king
THE MASTER OF BUTTING-IN, OFTEN COMPARED TO A CARTOON CHARACTER.
Dr. Kobayashi
HE POWERS UP WHEN HE ENCOUNTERS THUNDERBOLTS AND CHANGES INTO A MAD SCIENTIST.
Princess Shibayan
THE MISTRESS OF TONES.
"Hirachi" Hirakawa
A NATURAL-BORN DELINQUENT WHO NEVER SEEMS TO GET THE JOKE UNTIL IT'S TOO LATE. HE SNAPS WHEN INTERRUPTED.
Ryu Fujiwara
A HONG KONG MOVIE FAN WHO IS (BELIEVE IT OR NOT) TRYING TO GROW A CHINESE PIGTAIL.
Machine Yunokichi
THE ONLY IT MASTER IN THE WORKPLACE. THE BRAVE GUY WHO ALWAYS INTERRUPTS US.
Mr. K
A MYSTERIOUS FIGURE WHO STILL HASN'T MET THE OTHER MEMBERS OF THE STAFF.
Miss Eriko
A NATURALLY FANTASTIC GIRL WHO IS SLIGHTLY... ECCENTRIC.
THEY'RE ALL BUSY FREELANCERS WHO ARE OFTEN OFF WORKING AT OTHER SITES. KAZUNARI KAKEI SUMMONS THEM TO HELP HIM WHEN NEEDED!!

ALTHOUGH KAZUNARI KAKEI BOUGHT A VIDEO GAME CONSOLE, HE DIDN'T EVEN TOUCH IT FOR ALMOST A YEAR, LET ALONE BUY GAMES FOR IT. WHEN HE FINALLY PLAYED ONE, IT WAS A GAME SOMEBODY BROUGHT OVER.

LOITERING WITH INTENT
HO HUM
HIRACHI WAS WAITING FOR SOMEBODY AT THE STATION.
HE WAITED.
AND WAITED.
WHAT ARE YOU DOING HERE?
WHY ARE YOU LOITERING?
I'M WAITING...
...FOR SOMEBODY.
ZOOM
WHO? WHY? YOU'RE UP TO NO GOOD.
WHAT'S YOUR PROFESSION?
WHY AREN'T YOU AT WORK? OR AT SCHOOL?
INTERROGATION
UM...
SEE...
I'M JUST SAYING...
I SAID, "I'M A CARTOONIST, NOT A CROOK!" THEY SAID, "WHAT'S THE DIFFERENCE?"
HIRACHI WAS WEARING A TYPE OF SKI JACKET THAT DELINQUENTS WEAR IN JAPAN.
THE COPS THOUGHT HE LOOKED LIKE A PUNK.
SOB
...
SEXY GEEK?
To protect the subject's privacy, his image has been altered.
I'VE TOTALLY GOT HER.
SHE'S SO INTO ME!
WHAT HAPPENED TO THE GIRL FROM BEFORE?
OH, I'M NOT THAT INTO HER. IT'S ALL ABOUT THIS GIRL NOW.
SHE PLAYED HARD TO GET BUT I WORE HER DOWN.
YOU HAVE TWO GIRLS AT ONCE?
YOU'RE A TOTAL PLAYER.
MAYBE SOME PEOPLE FIND GEEKS TOO HOT...
DATING SIM GAME
SHUT UP!

DRAWN BY YOSHINON, QUEEN OF PAIN. AN EXPERT AT THE CARROT AND STICK. MEN ALL OVER THE WORLD ARE HER SLAVES.

DRAWN BY SHIBAYAN, WHO MAKES US GREAT SNACKS AND MEALS. THE LITTLE PRINCESS SHOWS OFF HER OTHER SKILLS IN HER WORK WITH TONES, WHICH ARE AS UNIFORM AND PRECISE AS IF A MACHINE CUT THEM.

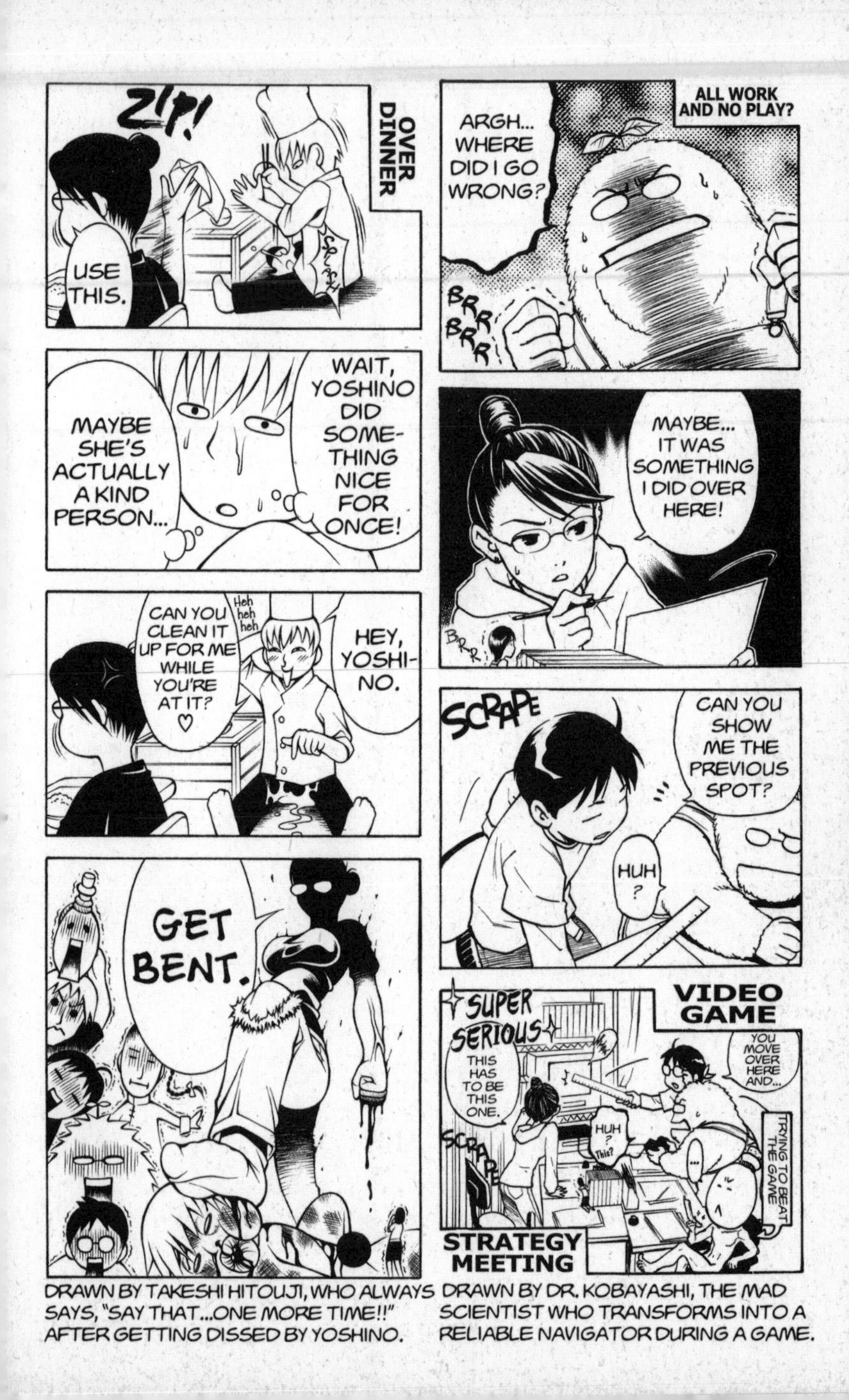

DRAWN BY TAKESHI HITOUJI, WHO ALWAYS SAYS, "SAY THAT...ONE MORE TIME!!" AFTER GETTING DISSED BY YOSHINO.

DRAWN BY DR. KOBAYASHI, THE MAD SCIENTIST WHO TRANSFORMS INTO A RELIABLE NAVIGATOR DURING A GAME.

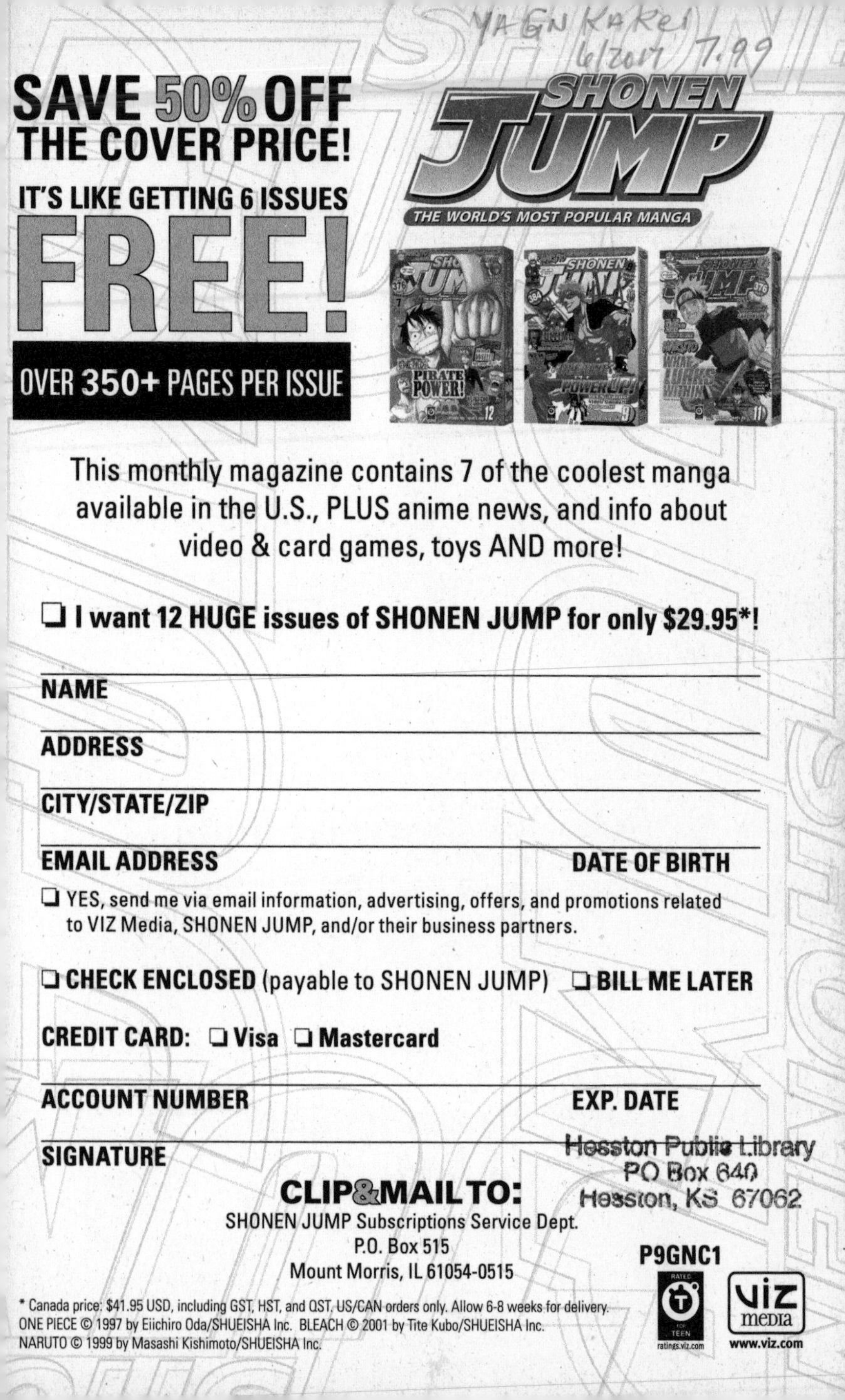